The Supporters' Guide to Football Programmes 1998

EDITOR
John Robinson

Third Edition

CONTENTS

FOREWORD

We wish to thank the administrative staffs of all 92 Premier and Football League clubs who have, without exception, cooperated in providing copies of their programmes for our use and in addition Ceri Sampson (cover artwork) and Paul Bruce (page layouts).

In addition, we wish to thank John Litster, the editor of Programme Monthly, for allowing us to use their reviews and, in addition, to reprint the article about the English Programme of the Year Awards.

Programme Monthly is Britain's foremost Football Programme magazine and we consider it a privilege to be associated with them in this way. However, the views expressed within the review section are entirely those of the reviewer and we do not necessarily agree with any opinions expressed therein.

John Robinson

British Library Cataloguing in Publication Data
A catalogue record for this book is available from the British Library
ISBN 1-86223-005-6

72, St. Peters' Avenue, Cleethorpes, N.E. Lincolnshire, DN35 8HU, England

Printed by Adlard Print & Typesetting Services, The Old School, The Green, Ruddington, Notts. NG11 6HH

Programme Monthly's English Programme of the Year Awards

Everything comes to those who wait, and for Leeds United this season sees the culmination of many years of producing excellent programmes. This season's magnificent Elland Road production has been judged to be the best in the country, ahead of the keenest competition ever from the Premiership clubs.

It is becoming increasingly difficult for clubs to improve their programmes, season on season, such is the high standard being achieved each year. The most programme buyers can reasonably expect is that clubs maintain standards, with those at the top freshening up their issues each season in the hope that the format, design and content chosen will all combine to produce something close to the perfect programme. That happened in 1996/97 for Leeds United, and up to a dozen other clubs could reasonably claim a similar achievement.

As well as recognising excellence, these awards annually review trends and the general health of programmes in the Premiership and Nationwide Leagues. The statistics confim the impression of some good news and some bad news in the batch of 1996/97 League programmes.

The good news is that quantity is up, by an average of 1.2 pages per programme. The issues are more colourful, with marginal increase in colour pages in the First Division and significant increases (of 25% and 22% respectively) in the Second and Third Divisions.

The bad news is that these improvements come at a price, albeit an increase (4.7%) which matches the rise in the number of pages. However, the impression that the commercial and advertising activities of clubs are making major inroads to the content of programmes is underlined by a 12% increase in the number of commercial pages across the board – up from an average of 12.6 pages per programme, to 13.5.

It would be a great shame if the continuing improvement in programme production and editorial standards is compromised by a reduction in the pages of pictures, statistics and text. One suspects that this will be a difficult trend to reverse.

To the programmes themselves, and firstly the area where most credit is due, the lower Leagues. All clubs have to make a conscious decision to allocate resources to make a programme that will stand out from the rest, and that is particularly so when crowds (and sales) are low. Here too, is where programme editors, that breed of unsung heroes, work hardest. With little or no monetary reward, their enthusiasm, energy, stamina and penmanship compensate for a lack of pages and colour. Remarkably, the statistics show that there has been an overall improvement in quantity and quality in the Third Division this season.

The creators of this season's programmes at the Uniteds of Hereford, Scunthorpe and Colchester can be justly proud of their efforts; marginally more so than their counterparts at Cambridge and Fulham. It is difficult enough to pick three programmes out of the top issues for the Third Division, without having to put them in order – suffice to say that the issues from Carlisle United, Exeter City and Hull City are quite outstanding.

Attendances (and sales) in the Second Division are often little better, but there is a perceptible leap in quantity. Gillingham and Watford have redesigned their programmes to excellent effect, as have Notts County and Bury. The Bristol Rovers programme is once again among the best in its Division, and the choice of best in the League falls to one of four clubs – Stockport County, Plymouth Argyle, Wrexham and Bristol City.

Another pair of eyes would justifiably come to a different conclusion, but it is to Wrexham's enormous credit that their programme is the best in the Second Division for the second successive year. It is difficult enough to make it to the very top, but to continue to improve to stay there takes very special qualities indeed, and the Wrexham programme team have these skills and abilities in abundance.

General improvement is once again the order of the day in the First Division, and the programmes of Tranmere Rovers, Queen's Park Rangers, Wolverhampton Wanderers, Oxford United and Norwich City are as good as there is across the land. As we move up the leagues, it becomes increasingly more difficult to choose a winner, and the impossible task falls amongst the programmes of Sheffield United, Swindon Town, Manchester City, Reading and Charlton Athletic.

Sheffield United have produced splendid programmes for many years, and they will undoubtedly win awards if they sustain such a high standard. The Reading programme would win an award for the most improved programme of the season, but by the tightest of margins, the splendid Manchester City programme wins the First Division award. It has been a difficult season for the Maine Road club, but they have kept faith with their programme, and their supporters, by improving upon their Premiership issue of last season.

There is not a bad programme in the Premiership – and the majority are practically flawless. There is ample consolation for those programmes which miss out on the top award – because many judges would make them top in their eyes. Certainly in that category are Middlesbrough, Sheffield Wednesday, Blackburn Rovers, Everton, Tottenham Hotspur, Aston Villa and West Ham United.

The short list from whom we chose the top three in the Premiership included Arsenal, Chelsea, Derby County, Sunderland, Newcastle United, Leeds United, Manchester United and Leicester City. One day Arsenal, judged this season to be third best, will win the top award, their consistent excellence certainly deserves it. Sunderland vie with Reading for the most improved programme in England this season, and in another year the Roker Park issue would have won the ultimate accolade.

The season belongs to the Leeds United programme, however, a massive 52-page production, larger than many and cheaper (at £1.70) than some. Design is exquisite, making full use of the club colours, and content is of the highest quality and admirable quantity.

Regular readers of this magazine will recognise the next two paragraphs – they are relevant this, and indeed every, season as they were last year.

"Programme Monthly" is no more qualified to judge such a "beauty contest" than anyone else, but we justify our participation in the annual round of awards by including all 92 club programmes, purchased at random through the season, in contrast to those awards which include only those programmes submitted by the clubs.

An enormous amount of work, ingenuity and effort goes into the production of just about every League club programme, and some of those involved surely deserve due recognition for their labours. The 4 programmes which were judged to be the best in their Divisions, and the 8 others singled out for special award, emerge from their subjective judgements – there can be no other way – but the widening of the awards to include all other programmes of merit reflects that the vast majority of League club programme editors deserve equal praise for their efforts this season.

Premiership

1ST – LEEDS UNITED
2ND – SUNDERLAND
3RD – ARSENAL

First Division

1ST – MANCHESTER CITY
2ND – READING
3RD – SHEFFIELD UNITED

Second Division

1ST – WREXHAM
2ND – STOCKPORT COUNTY
3RD – PLYMOUTH ARGYLE

Third Division

1ST – CARLISLE UNITED
2ND – EXETER CITY
3RD – HULL CITY

Other Premiership Awards

Very Highly Commended – Chelsea, Derby County, Newcastle United, Manchester United, Leicester City

Highly Commended – Sheffield Wednesday, Blackburn Rovers, Everton, Tottenham Hotspur, Aston Villa, West Ham United

Commended – Middlesbrough

Excellent – Southampton, Wimbledon, Nottingham Forest

Very Good – Coventry City, Liverpool

Other First Division Awards

Very Highly Commended – Q.P.R., Swindon Town, Wolverhampton Wanderers, Crystal Palace, Oxford United, Charlton Athletic, Norwich City

Highly Commended – Tranmere Rovers

Commended – Huddersfield Town, Barnsley

Excellent – Bolton Wanderers, Stoke City, West Bromwich Albion, Oldham Athletic

Very Good – Birmingham City, Bradford City, Ipswich Town, Port Vale, Portsmouth, Grimsby Town

Good – Southend United

Other Second Division Awards

Very Highly Commended – Bristol Rovers, Bury, Bristol City, Notts County

Highly Commended – Gillingham, Watford

Commended – Luton Town, Millwall, Bournemouth, Shrewsbury Town, Walsall, Wycombe Wanderers, York City

Excellent – Preston North End, Blackpool, Brentford, Burnley, Crewe Alexandra

Very Good – Rotherham United, Chesterfield, Peterborough United

Other Third Division Awards

Very Highly Commended – Fulham, Cambridge United

Highly Commended – Hereford United, Scunthorpe United, Colchester United

Commended – Doncaster Rovers, Northampton Town, Darlington, Rochdale

Excellent – Cardiff City, Wigan Athletic

Very Good – Barnet, Scarborough, Hartlepool United

Good – Mansfield Town, Swansea City, Brighton & Hove Albion, Leyton Orient, Lincoln City, Torquay United, Chester City

ARSENAL FC

Founded: 1886 **Admitted to League**: 1893
Former Name(s): Royal Arsenal (1886-1891), Woolwich Arsenal (1891-1914)
Ground Address: Arsenal Stadium, Avenell Road, Highbury, London N5 1BU
Phone Number: (0171) 704-4000

TECHNICAL INFORMATION

Size: 229mm x 151mm
Nº of Pages: 48
Price: £1.80
% Full Colour: 100%
% Adverts: 9.375%
% Content: 90.625%
Total Price per Page: 3.75p
Price per Page of Content: 4.14p
Printer: M Press (Sales) Ltd.
Editor: Kevin Connolly
Club Shop Phone: (0171) 704-4120

PROGRAMME MONTHLY REVIEW COMMENTS:

ARSENAL have tended to ring the design changes each season, but they have pretty much stuck with last season's successful format, and have spent the summer tidying up round the edges. The result is another excellent programme, full of interesting features, plenty of reading and lovely colour. A real contender for honours, as ever. Printed by M Press (Sales)

Aston Villa FC

Founded: 1874 **Admitted to League**: 1888
Former Name(s): None
Ground Address: Villa Park, Trinity Road, Birmingham, B6 6HE
Phone Number: (0121) 327-2299

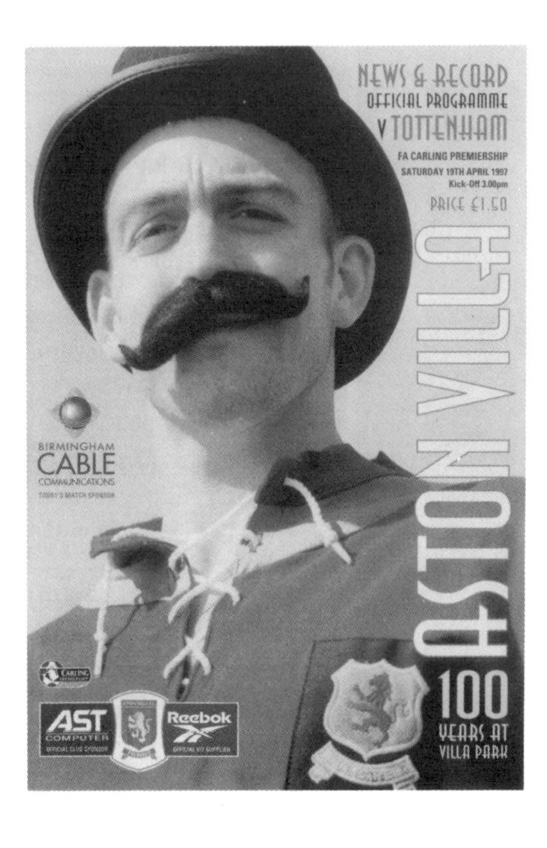

TECHNICAL INFORMATION

Size: 239mm x 170mm
Nº of Pages: 36 (inc. inset)
Price: £1.50
% Full Colour: 88.88%
% Adverts: 34.72%
% Content: 65.28%
Total Price per Page: 4.16p
Price per Page of Content: 4.69p
Printer: Polar Print Group Ltd
Editor: Denis Shaw, Mike Beddow, John Curtis & Rod Eves
Club Shop Phone: (0121) 327-2800

PROGRAMME MONTHLY REVIEW COMMENTS:

ASTON VILLA have stuck with the good old tried and trusted format – and why not. Economy of space has packed as many features and as much reading into this beautifully produced programme as you would find in programmes with half as many pages again. Full coverage of club affairs, features on club personalities – the programme is an object lesson in good programme production. Printed by Polar Print Group.

BARNET FC

Founded: 1888 **Admitted to League**: 1991
Former Name(s): Barnet Alston
Ground Address: Underhill Stadium, Barnet Lane, Barnet, Herts. EN5 2BE
Phone Number: (0181) 441-6932

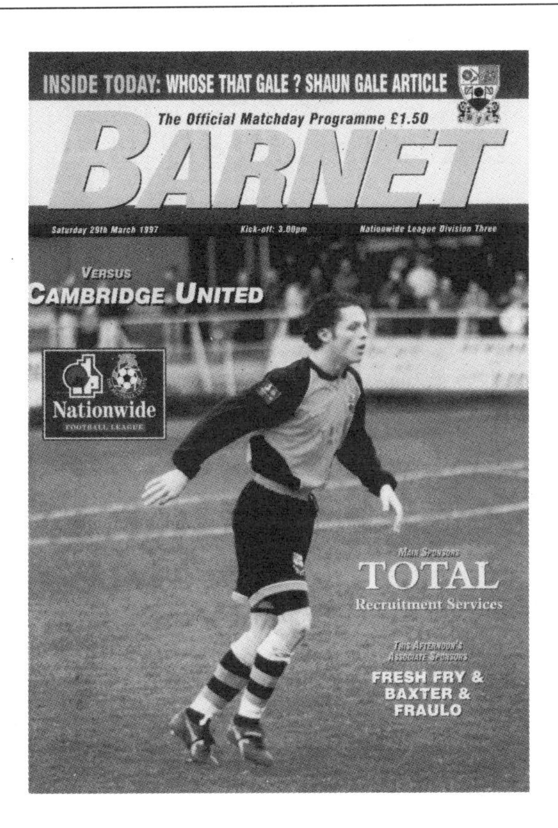

TECHNICAL INFORMATION

Size: 239mm x 167mm
Nº of Pages: 40
Price: £1.50
% Full Colour: 60%
% Adverts: 25%
% Content: 75%
Total Price per Page: 3.75p
Price per Page of Content: 5.00p
Printer: Queensway Publishing
Editor: Dave Bracegirdle
Club Shop Phone: (0181) 364-9601

PROGRAMME MONTHLY REVIEW COMMENTS:

The BARNET programme has made massive strides in terms of presentation over the last few years, and further improvement is evident this season. Colourful, ambitious in design, the format would not look out of place in a higher league. Modern print and design techniques can achieve so much with spot colour that the absence of full colour is hardly noticed in 40% of the programme. It is not quite the finished article – there are some rather large print sizes filling space, but if improvement at Underhill continues, this could be one of the programmes to watch in the near future.

BARNSLEY FC

Founded: 1887 **Admitted to League**: 1898
Former Name(s): Barnsley St. Peter's FC
Ground Address: Oakwell Ground, Grove Street, Barnsley S71 1ET
Phone Number: (01226) 211211

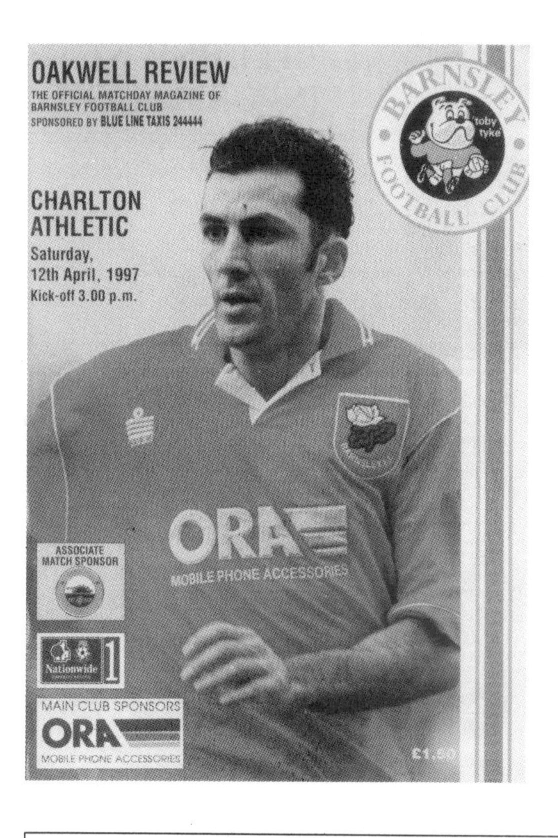

TECHNICAL INFORMATION

Size: 239mm x 170mm
Nº of Pages: 32
Price: £1.50
% Full Colour: 100%
% Adverts: 23.44%
% Content: 76.56%
Total Price per Page: 4.68p
Price per Page of Content: 6.12p
Printer: None credited
Editor: Keith Lodge
Club Shop Phone: (01226) 211211

PROGRAMME MONTHLY REVIEW COMMENTS:

Typical BARNSLEY good value for money, an excellent read, pleasant design and probably a whole set of happy buyers. There has always been an "intelligent" approach to programme content at Oakwell with some interesting and relevant features and thoughtful commentaries. "Oakwell Review" can be accused to underachieving, even complacency, but why spoil a nice programme and inflate the price in pursuit of vainglory?

BIRMINGHAM CITY FC

Founded: 1875 **Admitted to League**: 1892
Former Name(s): Small Heath Alliance FC (1875-88), Small Heath FC (1888-1905), Birmingham FC (1905-1945)
Ground Address: St. Andrew's, St. Andrew's Street, Birmingham B9 4NH
Phone Number: (0121) 772-0101

TECHNICAL INFORMATION

Size: 241mm x 169mm
Nº of Pages: 48
Price: £1.50
% Full Colour: 100%
% Adverts: 25%
% Content: 75%
Total Price per Page: 3.12p
Price per Page of Content: 4.17p
Printer: Colourplan, St. Helens
Editor: Ben Hallam
Club Shop Phone: (0121)772-0101 ext 8

PROGRAMME MONTHLY REVIEW COMMENTS:

Another extremely attractive programme from BIRMINGHAM CITY with a very pleasant layout and recurring design theme. There is strong text at the start of the issue, and again at the finish, but the middle segment of the programme is a succession of advertisements and commercial coverage. While this does not make it a bad programme, it will rule it out of the top honours, which is a pity for there is much to be admired in the City programme.

Blackburn Rovers FC

Founded: 1875 **Admitted to League**: 1888
Former Name(s): Blackburn Grammar School Old Boys FC
Ground Address: Ewood Park, Blackburn, Lancs. BB2 4JF
Phone Number: (01254) 698888

TECHNICAL INFORMATION

Size: 240mm x 169mm
Nº of Pages: 48
Price: £1.50
% Full Colour: 100%
% Adverts: 25%
% Content: 75%
Total Price per Page: 3.12p
Price per Page of Content: 4.17p
Printer: Langwood Ltd.
Editor: Peter White
Club Shop Phone: (01254) 672333

PROGRAMME MONTHLY REVIEW COMMENTS:

A splendid effort yet again from BLACKBURN ROVERS, who have had consistently good programmes for a great many years. Of modern, bright and colourful design, with good reading matter and a full range of features and information, this could be a dark horse for honours, One point in its favour is that a number of club-orientated adverts (boutique etc.) look as if they are features, and this innovative "disguise" gives a higher perception of value.

BLACKPOOL FC

Founded: 1887 **Admitted to League**: 1896
Former Name(s): Merged with Blackpool St. Johns 1887
Ground Address: Bloomfield Road, Blackpool, Lancashire FY1 6JJ
Phone Number: (01253) 405331

TECHNICAL INFORMATION

Size: 241mm x 167mm
Nº of Pages: 40
Price: £1.70
% Full Colour: 70%
% Adverts: 35.00%
% Content: 65.00%
Total Price per Page: 3.75p
Price per Page of Content: 5.76p
Printer: Colourplan Design and Print
Editor: Roger Harrison, Geoff Warburton
Club Shop Phone: (01253) 405331

PROGRAMME MONTHLY REVIEW COMMENTS:

The garnish tangerine has been toned down and the design of the BLACKPOOL issue is far easier on the eye, but this remains a mixed bag. There are some excellent aspects (forthright and opinionated articles of substantial reading) and the other side (very heavy advertising/commercial & some large print). A less frantic approach to page make up may have produced a more stunning programme, as the basic building blocks are there.

Bolton Wanderers FC

Founded: 1874 **Admitted to League**: 1888
Former Name(s): Christchurch FC (1874-77)
Ground Address: Reebok Stadium, Bolton, Lancashire
Phone Number: (01204) 389200

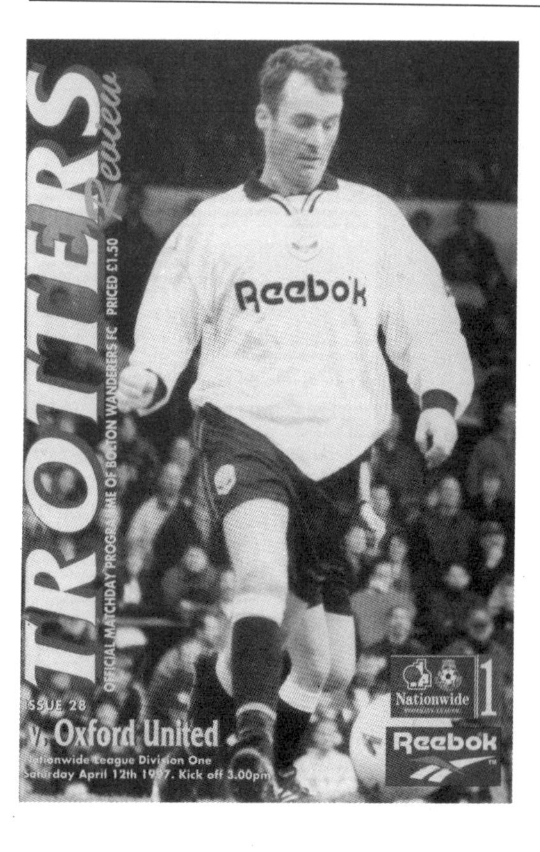

TECHNICAL INFORMATION

Size: 242mm x 167mm
Nº of Pages: 48
Price: £1.50
% Full Colour: 100%
% Adverts: 26.04%
% Content: 73.96%
Total Price per Page: 3.12p
Price per Page of Content: 4.22p
Printer: None credited
Editor: S. Marland
Club Shop Phone: (01204) 389200

PROGRAMME MONTHLY REVIEW COMMENTS:

BOLTON WANDERERS "Trotters Review" has the hardest of all transitions this season – From Premiership programme to First Division, but the change has been managed well and one could almost argue that there has been an improvement from last season. The second half of the programme is, however, something of a disappointment, with very little solid reading matter although pictorial coverage is good. That will probably consign it to last season's fate – very good, but not quite the finished article. No printer shown.

AFC BOURNEMOUTH

Founded: 1890 **Admitted to League**: 1923
Former Name(s): Boscombe St. Johns FC (1890-99), Boscombe FC (1899-1923), Bournemouth & Boscombe Athletic FC (1923-1972)
Ground Address: Dean Court, Bournemouth, Dorset
Phone Number: (01202) 395381

TECHNICAL INFORMATION

Size: 240mm x 163mm
Nº of Pages: 32
Price: £1.50
% Full Colour: 70%
% Adverts: 40.00%
% Content: 60.00%
Total Price per Page: 4.60p
Price per Page of Content: 7.89p
Printer: Cedar Press, Southampton
Editor: None credited
Club Shop Phone: (01202) 395381

PROGRAMME MONTHLY REVIEW COMMENTS:

BOURNEMOUTH have continued to produce an attractive and substantial programme and have taken steps to address last year's problem of thin reading matter. Advertising and commercial content is a little on the high side, but that must be understood in the context of the cash-strapped Second Division. An excellent programme, which just misses that extra "push" which would propel it to honours. In looks, this would not be out of place in a higher division.

BRADFORD CITY FC

Founded: 1903 **Admitted to League**: 1903
Former Name(s): None
Ground Address: Valley Parade, Bradford BD8 7DY
Phone Number: (01274) 773355

TECHNICAL INFORMATION

Size: 211mm x 149mm
Nº of Pages: 48
Price: £1.50
% Full Colour: 100%
% Adverts: 35.42%
% Content: 64.58%
Total Price per Page: 3.12p
Price per Page of Content: 4.83p
Printer: Edgar Woffenden Printers, Huddersfield
Editor: Kevin Mitchell
Club Shop Phone: (01274) 770012

PROGRAMME MONTHLY REVIEW COMMENTS:

There is a much improved "Claret and Amber" from BRADFORD CITY, in terms of colour and presentation in particular, resulting in an attractive issue and one of the few to retain faith in the small page size. The excellent array of features written by a range of contributors disguises some brevity in reading content, which is a shame because there are some fresh ideas and viewpoints. A pleasant programme which will please City supporters, but the high advertising and commercial content will prevent it from winning awards.

Brentford FC

Founded: 1889 **Admitted to League**: 1920

Former Name(s): None

Ground Address: Griffin Park, Braemar Road, Brentford, Middlesex TW8 0NT

Phone Number: (0181) 847-2511

TECHNICAL INFORMATION

Size: 239mm x 169mm

Nº of Pages: 32

Price: £1.50

% Full Colour: 100%

% Adverts: 28.12%

% Content: 71.88%

Total Price per Page: 4.68p

Price per Page of Content: 6.52p

Printer: Quay Design Ltd.

Editor: None credited

Club Shop Phone: (0181) 560-9836

PROGRAMME MONTHLY REVIEW COMMENTS:

A radical redesign has given the BRENTFORD programme a new look – but the underlying feeling and deep love of the club and its heritage remains, showing that modern styles, gloss and colour need not interfere with the soul of a club programme. Some nice new design ideas, a lot of general football articles and plenty on the Bees' History perhaps leaves a shortage of features on current personalities, betraying the comparatively small number of pages. Printed by Quay Design of Poole.

BRIGHTON & HOVE ALBION FC

Founded: 1900 **Admitted to League**: 1920
Former Name(s): Brighton and Hove Rangers FC (1900-1901)
Ground Address: Note: – the ground for the 1997-98 season was not decided at the time of going to print.
Phone Number: (01273) 778855

TECHNICAL INFORMATION

Size: 240mm x 170mm
Nº of Pages: 32
Price: £1.50
% Full Colour: 100%
% Adverts: 29.68%
% Content: 70.32%
Total Price per Page: 4.69p
Price per Page of Content: 6.66p
Printer: Bishops Printers, Portsmouth
Editor: None credited
Club Shop Phone: (01273) 778855

PROGRAMME MONTHLY REVIEW COMMENTS:

Alas poor BRIGHTON! It would be most unsporting to "put the boot in" programme wise, given the misfortunes which have been heaped on the poor Seagulls this season. Their programme starts off strongly, with substantial reading matter in the first few pages, but this is overtaken by adverts and commercial items as the staple approaches. By the end of a very colourful and attractive - looking programme, one has to conclude that it is not the longest read in the League. Moreover, 32 pages is a low number for a £1.50 price tag. Such a review is the least of this club's worries at the moment...

BRISTOL CITY FC

Founded: 1894 **Admitted to League**: 1901

Former Name(s): Bristol South End FC (1894-1897)

Ground Address: Ashton Gate, Winterstoke Road, Ashton Road, Bristol BS3 2EJ

Phone Number: (0117) 963-0630

TECHNICAL INFORMATION

Size: 245mm x 167mm

Nº of Pages: 36

Price: £1.50

% Full Colour: 100%

% Adverts: 25%

% Content: 75%

Total Price per Page: 4.17p

Price per Page of Content: 5.56p

Printer: Farrow (Printers) Limited

Editor: None credited

Club Shop Phone: (0117) 930-0661

PROGRAMME MONTHLY REVIEW COMMENTS:

For BRISTOL CITY, the same verdict as last year – ignore first impressions of a slim volume, this is a smashing programme. Delightfully designed and produced, with as few advert/commercial pages as you are likely to find in the League, and plenty to read – a real gem. Perhaps the winning feature of this programme is its simplicity, with no over elaboration of design or features, just a clean-cut substantial read.

BRISTOL ROVERS FC

Founded: 1883 **Admitted to League**: 1920
Former Name(s): Black Arabs FC (1883-1884), Eastville Rovers FC (1884-1896), Bristol Eastville Rovers FC (1896-1897)
Ground Address: The Memorial Ground, Filton Avenue, Horfield, Bristol
Phone Number: (0117) 977-2000

TECHNICAL INFORMATION

Size: 243mm x 175mm
Nº of Pages: 52
Price: £1.50
% Full Colour: 100%
% Adverts: 44.23%
% Content: 55.77%
Total Price per Page: 3.12p
Price per Page of Content: 5.17p
Printer: Sports Programme Promotions
Editor: None credited
Club Shop Phone: (0117) 961-1772

PROGRAMME MONTHLY REVIEW COMMENTS:

An earlier edition of PM carried a review of a BRISTOL ROVERS programme for a special fixture, and the club has kindly forwarded a copy of a regular League match issue, a more accurate picture of how programmes are faring at The Memorial Ground. Very well indeed is the verdict, with an expansive and impressive modern issue, full of features and reading material. This is a colourful and attractive issue, although design is a little basic in places, but the emphasis has been placed on full features, resulting in a value for money production. Rovers are very much back on form programme-wise with this issue which, in deference to the comparatively recent transfer from A5 size, may take a season or two to reach full maturity. Designed and produced by Sports Programme Promotions.

BURNLEY FC

Founded: 1882 **Admitted to League**: 1888

Former Name(s): Burnley Rovers FC

Ground Address: Turf Moor, Brunshaw Road, Burnley, Lancashire BB10 4BX

Phone Number: (01282) 700000

TECHNICAL INFORMATION

Size: 238mm x 160mm
Nº of Pages: 48
Price: £1.50
% Full Colour: 100%
% Adverts: 43.75%
% Content: 56.25%
Total Price per Page: 3.12p
Price per Page of Content: 5.55p
Printer: Mercer Print
Editor: J. Stringer
Club Shop Phone: (01282) 700000

PROGRAMME MONTHLY REVIEW COMMENTS:

Plenty of pages in the BURNLEY issue – plenty of adverts and commercial coverage, not helped by player sponsorship spead throughout the programme. Nevertheless a pleasant programme, nicely turned out in claret and sky blue with the minimum of fuss. No better than that, however, and a little bit underwhelming with a stortage of current club features spoiling an otherwise worthy effort.

Bury FC

Founded: 1885 **Admitted to League**: 1894
Former Name(s): None
Ground Address: Gigg Lane, Bury, Lancashire BL9 9HR
Phone Number: (0161) 764-4881

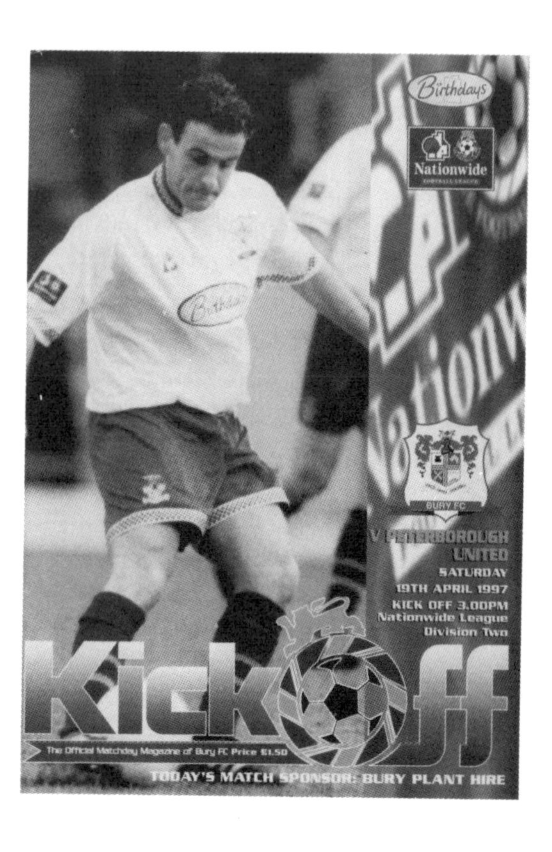

TECHNICAL INFORMATION

Size: 241mm x 167mm
Nº of Pages: 40
Price: £1.50
% Full Colour: 100%
% Adverts: 30%
% Content: 70%
Total Price per Page: 3.75p
Price per Page of Content: 5.37p
Printer: Colourplan Design and Print
Editor: None credited
Club Shop Phone: (0161) 764-4881

PROGRAMME MONTHLY REVIEW COMMENTS:

Lovely stuff from BURY with an extremely pleasant looking programme. A low percentage of full colour, but the blue and red spot colour pages are nicely laid out and tastefully designed to compensate. Content is first class, with plenty to read in a wide range of interesting features. The Bury programme has been "bubbling under" for some years, but it has flowered this season into a potential award winner.

CAMBRIDGE UNITED FC

Founded: 1919 **Admitted to League**: 1970
Former Name(s): Abbey United FC (1919-1949)
Ground Address: Abbey Stadium, Newmarket Road, Cambridge CB5 8LN
Phone Number: (01223) 566500

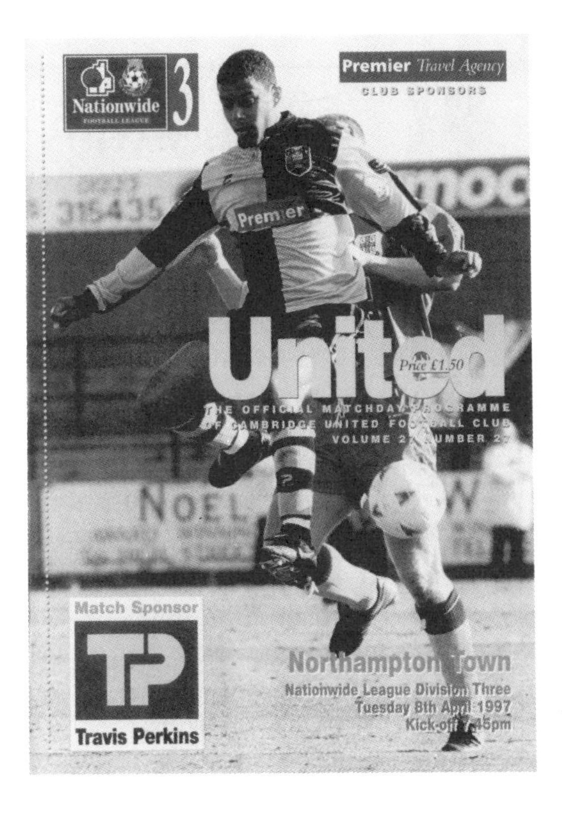

TECHNICAL INFORMATION

Size: 239mm x 169mm
Nº of Pages: 32
Price: £1.50
% Full Colour: 81.25%
% Adverts: 29.12%
% Content: 70.88%
Total Price per Page: 4.69p
Price per Page of Content: 6.52p
Printer: Queensway Publishing, London
Editor: Andrew Pincher
Club Shop Phone: (01223) 566503

PROGRAMME MONTHLY REVIEW COMMENTS:

Another splendid programme from CAMBRIDGE UNITED despite working within tight financial constraints and having to maximise given resources. There's nothing too fancy or bulky about this issue, but advertising and commercial items have been held at bay, design is pleasant and unobtrusive, reproduction and paper quality is of the best, and there is plenty to read. What more do you want? An object lesson in producing a first class programme on small gates.

Cardiff City FC

Founded: 1899 **Admitted to League**: 1920
Former Name(s): Riverside FC (1899-1910)
Ground Address: Ninian Park, Sloper Road, Cardiff CF1 8SX
Phone Number: (01222) 398636

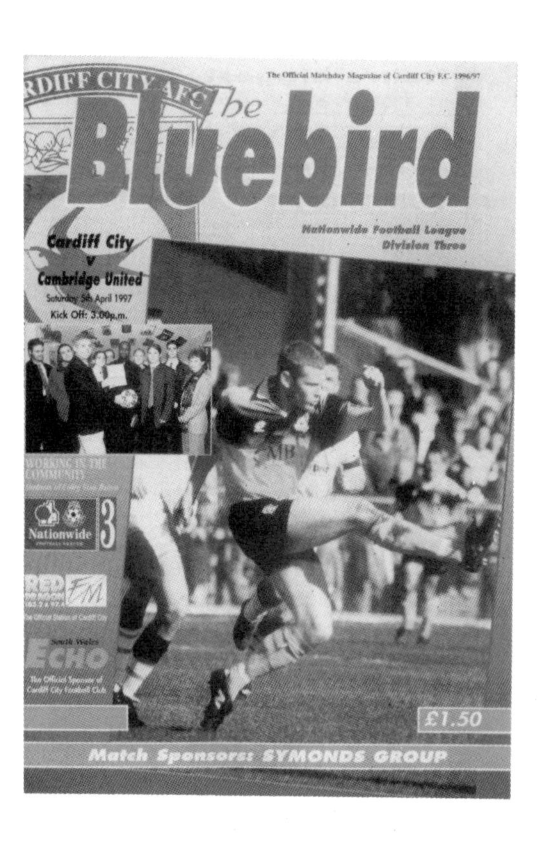

TECHNICAL INFORMATION

Size: 244mm x 164mm
Nº of Pages: 32
Price: £1.50
% Full Colour: 100%
% Adverts: 28.12%
% Content: 71.88%
Total Price per Page: 4.69p
Price per Page of Content: 6.52p
Printer: PRS Associates, Bristol
Editor: None Credited
Club Shop Phone: (01222) 398636

PROGRAMME MONTHLY REVIEW COMMENTS:

The CARDIFF CITY programme has had its ups and downs in recent years, and this season's version can be looked upon as an improvement, and hopefully the start of an upward gradient. The programme looks first class, although there is some economy in the use of colour, but it remains a quick read in comparison to others and in that context, and with its 32 pages, it is expensive at £1.50.

CARLISLE UNITED FC

Founded: 1903 **Admitted to League**: 1928
Former Name(s): Formed by amalgamation of Shaddon Gate Utd FC and Carlisle Red Rose FC
Ground Address: Brunton Park, Warwick Road, Carlisle CA1 1LL
Phone Number: (01228) 26237

TECHNICAL INFORMATION

Size: 238mm x 159mm
Nº of Pages: 32
Price: £1.40
% Full Colour: 100%
% Adverts: 21.87%
% Content: 78.13%
Total Price per Page: 4.38p
Price per Page of Content: 5.60p
Printer: Mercer Print (UK) Limited, Accrington
Editor: Paul Newton & Mark Knighton
Club Shop Phone: (01228) 24014

PROGRAMME MONTHLY REVIEW COMMENTS:

CARLISLE UNITED have maintained the improvement shown in last season's programme, and this year's is a first class effort. Packed with interesting and authoritative features, beautifully presented in a bright, colourful and tasteful format, this is one of the best in the lower Leagues.

CHARLTON ATHLETIC FC

Founded: 1905 **Admitted to League**: 1921
Former Name(s): None
Ground Address: The Valley, Floyd Road, Charlton, London SE7 8BL
Phone Number: (0181) 333-4000

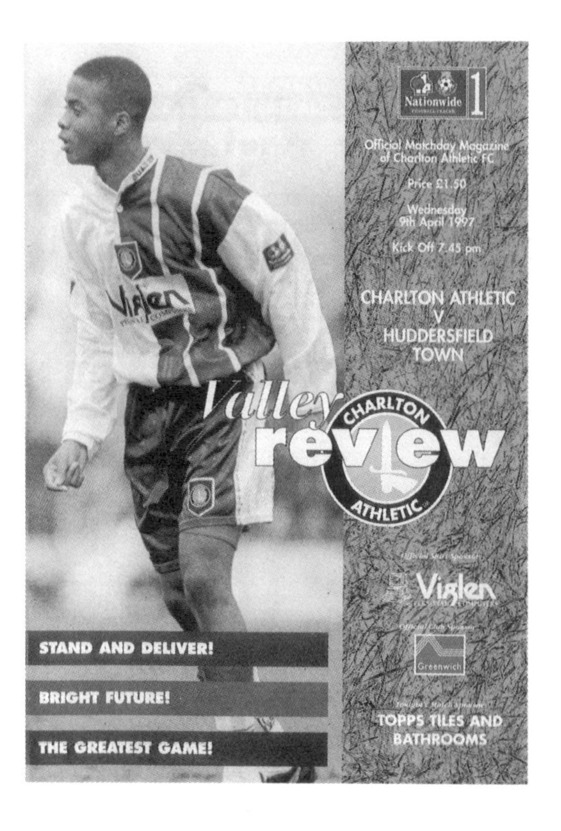

TECHNICAL INFORMATION

Size: 240mm x 168mm
Nº of Pages: 40
Price: £1.50
% Full Colour: 100%
% Adverts: 35.00%
% Content: 65.00%
Total Price per Page: 3.75p
Price per Page of Content: 4.54p
Printer: Morganprint, Blackheath
Editor: None credited
Club Shop Phone: (0181) 333-4035

PROGRAMME MONTHLY REVIEW COMMENTS:

Perhaps this is the year in which the consistently excellent CHARLTON ATHLETIC programme will win a long-deserved award. Beautifully produced making excellent use of the club colours, and full of interesting and informative features. It is comparatively heavy on adverts, but the text is compact and well laid out. Excellent value for money and (once again) a real contender for honours. Design by Image Directors.

CHELSEA FC

Founded: 1905 **Admitted to League**: 1905
Former Name(s): None
Ground Address: Stamford Bridge, Fulham Road, London SW6 1HS
Phone Number: (0171) 385-5545

TECHNICAL INFORMATION

Size: 238mm x 164mm
Nº of Pages: 56
Price: £2.00
% Full Colour: 100%
% Adverts: 14.28%
% Content: 85.72%
Total Price per Page: 3.57p
Price per Page of Content: 4.17p
Printer: Thruxton Press
Editor: Neil Barnett
Club Shop Phone: (0171) 381-4569

PROGRAMME MONTHLY REVIEW COMMENTS:

CHELSEA – Last season's award winner, and for this season's review... just refer to last season's. Simply superb once again, with the added bonus of no price increase. It's almost textbook stuff, with near perfection in design, presentation, spread and scope of features, club news, past features and a marvellous visitors summary. You are defied to deny that this is excellent value for money.

CHESTER CITY FC

Founded: 1884 **Admitted to League**: 1931
Former Name(s): Chester FC
Ground Address: The Deva Stadium, Bumpers Lane, Chester CH1 4LT
Phone Number: (01244) 371376

TECHNICAL INFORMATION

Size: 240mm x 167mm
Nº of Pages: 32
Price: £1.50
% Full Colour: 100%
% Adverts: 40.62%
% Content: 59.38%
Total Price per Page: 4.69p
Price per Page of Content: 7.89p
Printer: Colourplan, St. Helens
Editor: D. Andrews
Club Shop Phone: (01244) 390243

PROGRAMME MONTHLY REVIEW COMMENTS:

The CHESTER CITY programme is opened with some relish each season as it consistently "outscored" the team in terms of its comparative merits. The very attractive use of club colours remains, and there is the usual strong historical content, but advertising has intruded to an alarming extent, and one is left with the feeling that there is too little concerning contemporay club matters within this attractive issue. This despite a couple of enteraining and information "supporters-orientated" articles. It is disappointing that the high standards for some years by the Chester programme have been compromised.

CHESTERFIELD FC

Founded: 1866 **Admitted to League**: 1899
Former Name(s): Chesterfield Town FC
Ground Address: Recreation Ground, Saltergate, Chesterfield S40 4SX
Phone Number: (01246) 209765

TECHNICAL INFORMATION

Size: 209mm x 147mm
Nº of Pages: 36
Price: £1.50
% Full Colour: 100%
% Adverts: 50.00%
% Content: 50.00%
Total Price per Page: 4.17p
Price per Page of Content: 6.66p
Printer: Brampton Print & Design
Editor: Jessica Eyre
Club Shop Phone: (01246) 231535

PROGRAMME MONTHLY REVIEW COMMENTS:

The CHESTERFIELD – issue is bigger in page size, but not as good as the smaller issues from Saltergate in recent seasons. This is a big ideas programme with too many adverts, too little of substance and an over-simplified design, particularly in the non-colour pages. There are a lot of columnists, with various coaches and club officials having their say, but the programme appears to be without a soul. Designed by Broadleaf Design and Marketing.

COLCHESTER UNITED FC

Founded: 1937 **Admitted to League**: 1950
Former Name(s): The Eagles
Ground Address: Layer Road Ground, Colchester CO2 7JJ
Phone Number: (01206) 508800

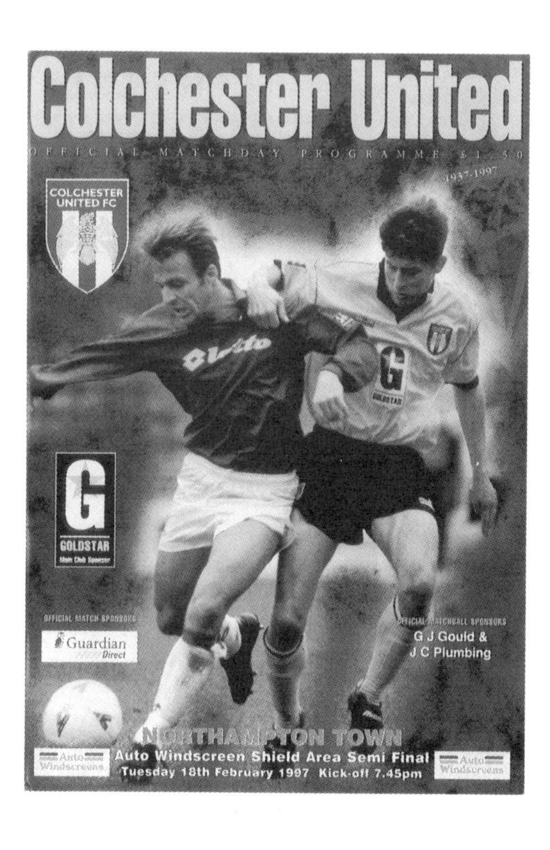

TECHNICAL INFORMATION

Size: 240mm x 168mm
Nº of Pages: 40
Price: £1.50
% Full Colour: 100%
% Adverts: 35%
% Content: 65%
Total Price per Page: 3.75p
Price per Page of Content: 5.77p
Printer: Queensway Publishing, London
Editor: None Credited
Club Shop Phone: (01206) 508800

PROGRAMME MONTHLY REVIEW COMMENTS:

Nice issue from COLCHESTER UNITED. Extremely modern and attractive, if a little reminiscent of others, with a nice balance between small features, and more wordy pieces. While the format has lost the "homely feel" of years gone by, it is more than compensated by colour and polish. A high advertising/commercial content may preclude it from honours, but this remains an issue to be proud of.

COVENTRY CITY FC

Founded: 1883 **Admitted to League**: 1919
Former Name(s): Singers FC (1883-1898)
Ground Address: Highfield Road Stadium, King Richard Street, Coventry, CV2 4FW
Phone Number: (01203) 234000

TECHNICAL INFORMATION

Size: 209mm x 148mm
Nº of Pages: 48
Price: £1.80
% Full Colour: 100%
% Adverts: 31.25%
% Content: 68.75%
Total Price per Page: 3.75p
Price per Page of Content: 4.29p
Printer: None credited
Editor: Mike Williams
Club Shop Phone: (01203) 234030

PROGRAMME MONTHLY REVIEW COMMENTS:

The COVENTRY CITY programme is a welcome change from the large size issues favoured by just about every League club, so praise to City for preferring the old-fashioned A5 format. To rise above the larger programmes of contemporaries – with the same number of pages – requires a very special effort in content and unfortunately this is not forthcoming, although what is provided is fairly substantial and well designed. There remains a slight hint of "dullness" in presentation, however, and the price is somewhat excessive.

Crewe Alexandra FC

Founded: 1877 **Admitted to League**: 1892
Former Name(s): None
Ground Address: Gresty Road Ground, Crewe, Cheshire CW2 6EB
Phone Number: (01270) 213014

TECHNICAL INFORMATION

Size: 297mm x 210mm
Nº of Pages: 20
Price: £1.50
% Full Colour: 20%
% Adverts: 27.5%
% Content: 72.5%
Total Price per Page: 7.50p
Price per Page of Content: 10.34p
Printer: None credited
Editor: Harold Finch
Club Shop Phone: (01270) 213014

PROGRAMME MONTHLY REVIEW COMMENTS:

"The Alexandra Football Special" is as different from the traditional CREWE ALEXANDRA programme as you would possibly imagine – brochure page size, high gloss paper and excellent print quality. This is, of course, refreshingly different, which probably disguises the high advertising content and the immodest price of what is the equivalent of 32 A5 pages. Nonetheless, this is a splendid looking production with some substantial and quality reading. All being well with the world is testified by "An Individual View" being written by – Harold Finch.

CRYSTAL PALACE FC

Founded: 1905 **Admitted to League**: 1920
Former Name(s): None
Ground Address: Selhurst Park, London SE25 6PU
Phone Number: (0181) 768-6000

TECHNICAL INFORMATION

Size: 240mm x 169mm
Nº of Pages: 56
Price: £2.00
% Full Colour: 100%
% Adverts: 28.57%
% Content: 71.43%
Total Price per Page: 3.57p
Price per Page of Content: 5p
Printer: Morganprint Limited
Editor: None credited
Club Shop Phone: (0181) 768-6100

PROGRAMME MONTHLY REVIEW COMMENTS:

A massive production from CRYSTAL PALACE which is quite possibly superior to anything they produced when they were in the Premiership. The emphasis is on content; design while pleasant and effective, is simple and uncomplicated. The amount of reading is almost without precedent in any programme this season and needless to say no aspect of club affairs, or features, is left uncovered. Outstanding value for money.

DARLINGTON FC

Founded: 1883 **Admitted to League**: 1921

Former Name(s): None

Ground Address: Feethams Ground, Darlington DL1 5JB

Phone Number: (01325) 465097

TECHNICAL INFORMATION

Size: 210mm x 149mm

№ of Pages: 32

Price: £1.50

% Full Colour: 100%

% Adverts: 34.37%

% Content: 65.63%

Total Price per Page: 4.69p

Price per Page of Content: 7.14p

Printer: Mawes Talbot Print

Editor: Ken Lavery

Club Shop Phone: (01325) 465097

PROGRAMME MONTHLY REVIEW COMMENTS:

The DARLINGTON programme may not be an award winner, but it is one of the most pleasant and attractive around this season. Design is easy on the eye, with non-full colour pages suffering nothing from the subtle use of red and black. Features provide a good read and are varied and imaginitive. It is a smashing programme, and arguably the best yet from the Feethams.

Derby County FC

Founded: 1884 **Admitted to League**: 1888

Former Name(s): None

Ground Address: Pride Park Stadium, Derby

Phone Number: (01332) 340105

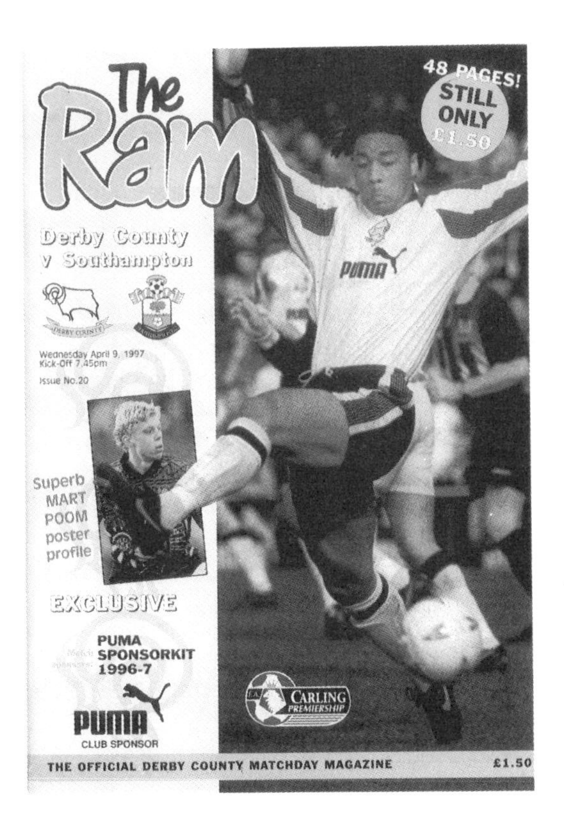

TECHNICAL INFORMATION

Size: 240mm x 170mm

Nº of Pages: 48

Price: £1.50

% Full Colour: 100%

% Adverts: 20.83%

% Content: 79.17%

Total Price per Page: 3.12p

Price per Page of Content: 3.94p

Printer: CBE 2000, Birmingham

Editor: None credited

Club Shop Phone: (01332) 340105

PROGRAMME MONTHLY REVIEW COMMENTS:

DERBY COUNTY have reacted to promotion to the Premiership by improving their programme and the result is a well-rounded, substantial issue that will stand comparison with any in the country. Attractively designed, well presented and full of features and information on the club – a splendid production.

DONCASTER ROVERS FC

Founded: 1879 **Admitted to League**: 1901

Former Name(s): None

Ground Address: Belle Vue, Bawtry Road, Doncaster DN4 5HT

Phone Number: (01302) 539441

TECHNICAL INFORMATION

Size: 240mm x 170mm

Nº of Pages: 40

Price: £1.50

% Full Colour: 100%

% Adverts: 27.5%

% Content: 72.5%

Total Price per Page: 3.75p

Price per Page of Content: 5.17p

Printer: Askew Design & Print, Doncaster

Editor: Bernard Jordan

Club Shop Phone: (01302) 535093

PROGRAMME MONTHLY REVIEW COMMENTS:

Another splendid looking programme from DONCASTER ROVERS, maintaining the high standards developed over the last few years. Alternate double pages are full colour and spot red, but the issue does not suffer from this, as design is strong throughout. Reading is just a little on the light side, with small-sized features and some space filling and large print. Nonetheless, a good programme with sufficient variety of content to please its buyers.

Everton FC

Founded: 1878 **Admitted to League**: 1888

Former Name(s): St. Domingo's FC (1878-1879)

Ground Address: Goodison Park, Goodison Road, Liverpool L4 4EL

Phone Number: (0151) 330-2200

TECHNICAL INFORMATION

Size: 242mm x 168mm

Nº of Pages: 44

Price: £1.70

% Full Colour: 100%

% Adverts: 18.18%

% Content: 81.82%

Total Price per Page: 3.86p

Price per Page of Content: 4.72p

Printer: Colourplan, St. Helens

Editor: None credited

Club Shop Phone: (0151) 330-2333

PROGRAMME MONTHLY REVIEW COMMENTS:

EVERTON have produced excellent programmes for many years, and this season is no exception. Indeed the changes in design and format have freshened the Goodison issue and have arguably improved it. Massive amount of reading, nicely presented in a colourful and modern style, with a good mixture of club information, current features and strong historical content. An added bonus is the very small proportion of advertising/commercial pages, making this excellent value for money, albeit at a premium over the £1.50 norm. As ever, a contender for honours.

EXETER CITY FC

Founded: 1904 **Admitted to League**: 1920
Former Name(s): Formed by amalgamation of St. Sidwell United FC and Exeter United FC
Ground Address: St. James Park, Exeter EX4 6PX
Phone Number: (01392) 254073

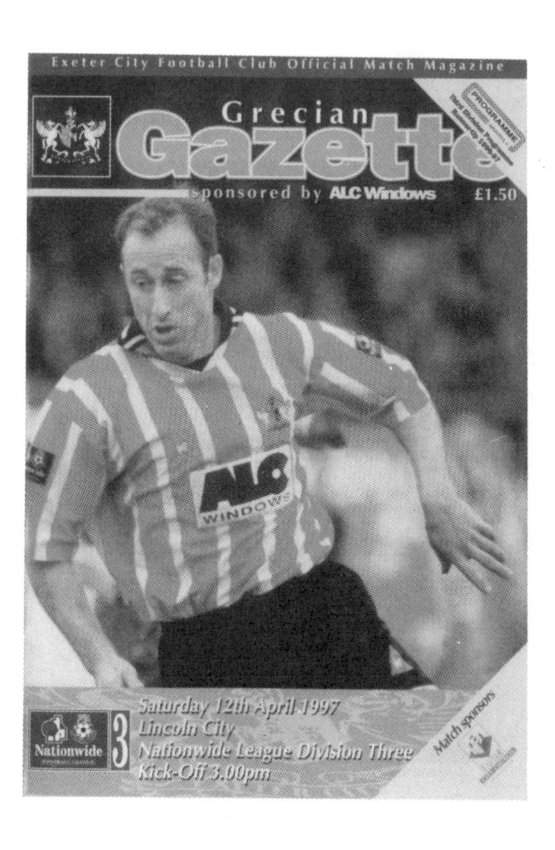

TECHNICAL INFORMATION

Size: 240mm x 168mm
Nº of Pages: 40
Price: £1.50
% Full Colour: 20%
% Adverts: 35%
% Content: 65%
Total Price per Page: 3.75p
Price per Page of Content: 5.77p
Printer: Kingfisher Print and Design, Totnes
Editor: Mike Blackstone
Club Shop Phone: (01392) 254073

PROGRAMME MONTHLY REVIEW COMMENTS:

Another EXETER CITY masterpiece from the pen of Mike Blackstone, with information and features crammed into this highly attractive issue. Comprehensive coverage of all aspects of club affairs with surely the smallest and most compact type-size in the country. The few colour pages have been sensibly deployed and the monotone ones are attractively designed. Once again, this will not be far away from honours.

FULHAM FC

Founded: 1879 **Admitted to League**: 1907

Former Name(s): Fulham St. Andrew's FC (1879-1898)

Ground Address: Craven Cottage, Stevenage Road, Fulham, London SW6 6HH

Phone Number: (0171) 736-6561

TECHNICAL INFORMATION

Size: 241mm x 169mm

Nº of Pages: 32

Price: £1.50

% Full Colour: 100%

% Adverts: 18.75%

% Content: 81.25%

Total Price per Page: 4.68p

Price per Page of Content: 5.77p

Printer: Morganprint Blackheath Limited

Editor: None credited

Club Shop Phone: (0171) 736-3292

PROGRAMME MONTHLY REVIEW COMMENTS:

FULHAM have at least succumbed to the inevitabilities of the bottom Division and their programme is not as substantial as it was before. It remains extremely attractive, and the reading material remains substantial and information. Against the comparatively low number of pages is the even lower advertising ratio, and the result is one of the best programmes in the lower Leagues. The issue reviewed had a four page black and white photo supplement to commemorate a century of matches at Craven Cottage.

GILLINGHAM FC

Founded: 1893 **Admitted to League**: 1920
Former Name(s): New Brompton FC (1898-1913)
Ground Address: Priestfield Stadium, Redfern Ave., Gillingham, Kent ME7 4DD
Phone Number: (01634) 851854

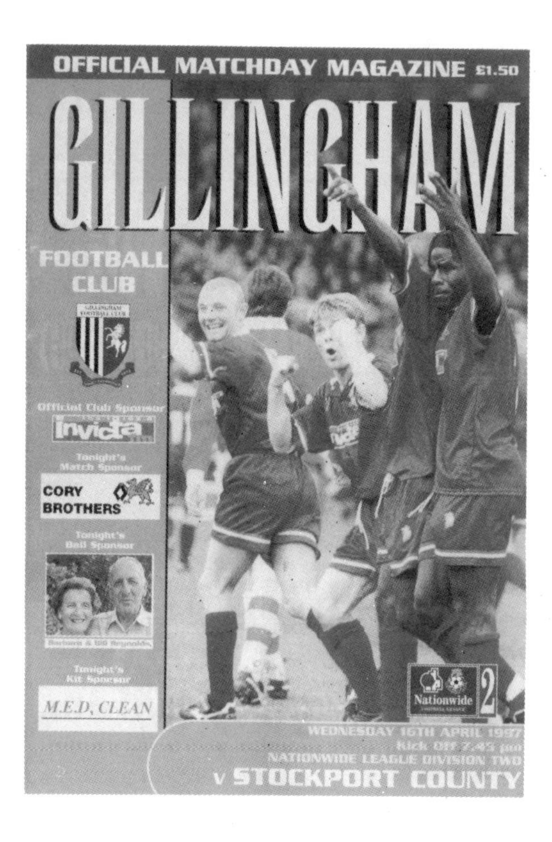

TECHNICAL INFORMATION

Size: 242mm x 170mm
Nº of Pages: 48
Price: £1.50
% Full Colour: 100%
% Adverts: 41.67%
% Content: 58.33%
Total Price per Page: 3.12p
Price per Page of Content: 5.36p
Printer: Morganprint Blackheath Limited
Editor: Matt Davison
Club Shop Phone: (01634) 851462

PROGRAMME MONTHLY REVIEW COMMENTS:

A gloriously colourful and extremely well designed issue from GILLINGHAM, which would not be out of place in a higher Division. To quibble, design and photos take over a lot of space that might otherwise be devoted to the written word, and commerical/advertising certainly prevails after the staple. That said, it is a continuous improvement from last season, and a splendid looking programme with some first class features.

GRIMSBY TOWN FC

Founded: 1878 **Admitted to League**: 1892
Former Name(s): Grimsby Pelham FC (1879)
Ground Address: Blundell Park, Cleethorpes, N.E. Lincolnshire DN35 7PY
Phone Number: (01472) 697111

TECHNICAL INFORMATION

Size: 245mm x 164mm
Nº of Pages: 32
Price: £1.50
% Full Colour: 100%
% Adverts: 34.37%
% Content: 65.63%
Total Price per Page: 4.68p
Price per Page of Content: 7.14p
Printer: Colourplan
Editor: None credited
Club Shop Phone: (01472) 697111

PROGRAMME MONTHLY REVIEW COMMENTS:

Colourplan have waved their magic wand over the GRIMSBY TOWN programme, which is very much improved on the fairly chronic issues of recent seasons. Design is very good indeed, emphasising the unpromising club colours (black and white) while retaining a colourful look. Content has improved, making it a far better read for the high price . There remains some way to go, with still-intrusive advertising, and only 32 pages to work with, but this is a vast improvement and is to be commended.

HARTLEPOOL UNITED FC

Founded: 1908 **Admitted to League**: 1921
Former Name(s): Hartlepools United FC (1908-1968), Hartlepool FC (1968-1977)
Ground Address: Victoria Ground, Clarence Road, Hartlepool TS24 8BZ
Phone Number: (01429) 272584

TECHNICAL INFORMATION

Size: 210mm x 148mm
Nº of Pages: 32
Price: £1.30
% Full Colour: 25%
% Adverts: 34.37%
% Content: 66.73%
Total Price per Page: 4.06p
Price per Page of Content: 6.19p
Printer: Mawers Talbot Print, Darlington
Editor: None credited
Club Shop Phone: (01429) 222077

PROGRAMME MONTHLY REVIEW COMMENTS:

HARTLEPOOL have economised on pages and colour this season, with an otherwise attractive issue which makes the most of its unpromising resources with pleasant use of two colour printing. There is a reasonable volume of reading material, with the emphasis on club information, so closer inspection refutes the first impression that United have failed to apply effort and imagination to their programme. There is acknowledgement of the modesty of the enterprise with a £1.30 cover price.

HEREFORD UNITED FC

Founded: 1924 **Admitted to League**: 1972
Former Name(s): None
Ground Address: Edgar Street, Hereford HR4 9JU
Phone Number: (01432) 276666

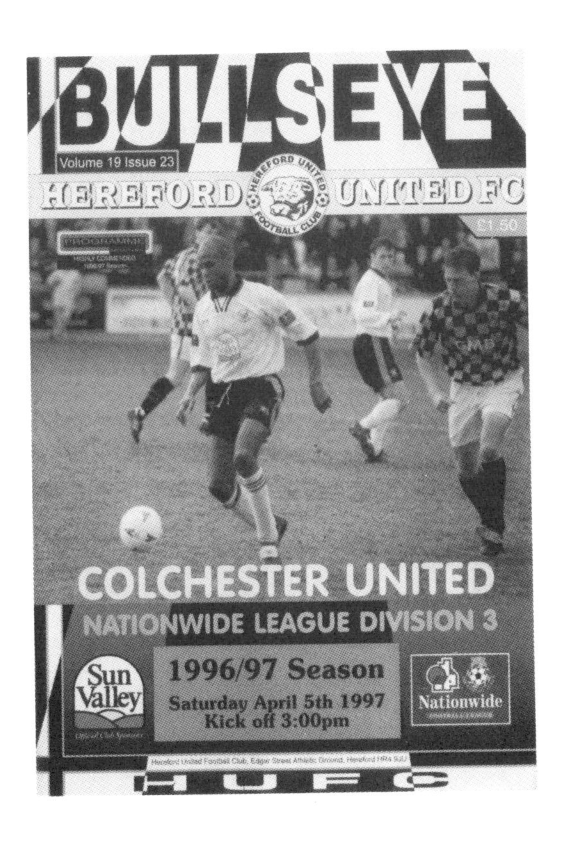

TECHNICAL INFORMATION

Size: 240mm x 167mm
Nº of Pages: 48
Price: £1.50
% Full Colour: 40%
% Adverts: 47.92%
% Content: 52.08%
Total Price per Page: 3.12p
Price per Page of Content: 6.00p
Printer: Print Logic Ltd.
Editor: Keith Hall
Club Shop Phone: (01432) 276666

PROGRAMME MONTHLY REVIEW COMMENTS:

Full marks to HEREFORD UNITED for maintaining last season's high standard of issue, despite Third Division status. The quantity of text is commendable, even allowing for an extremely high number of advertising/commercial pages, and this is likely to be a programme which will please home supporters. Adverts are extremely intrusive, unfortunately, and this detracts from the issue along with a standard design that is not to everyone's taste.

HUDDERSFIELD TOWN FC

Founded: 1908 **Admitted to League**: 1910
Former Name(s): None
Ground Address: The Sir Alfred McAlpine Stadium, Leeds Road, Huddersfield
Phone Number: (01484) 420335

TECHNICAL INFORMATION

Size: 240mm x 171mm
Nº of Pages: 40
Price: £1.50
% Full Colour: 100%
% Adverts: 15.00%
% Content: 85.00%
Total Price per Page: 3.75p
Price per Page of Content: 4.41p
Printer: Walker Design and Print, Huddersfield
Editor: Alan Stevenson, Will Venters
Club Shop Phone: (01484) 534867

PROGRAMME MONTHLY REVIEW COMMENTS:

Plenty to read in the HUDDERSFIELD TOWN programme, with the emphasis on information and entertaining text. There are strong articles on Town history and a series on the history of the club's programmes, and strong representation from club officials in the pages. Design is slightly disappointing, in that it is basic and rather plain, but this remains a first class read and a good value programme.

HULL CITY FC

Founded: 1904 **Admitted to League**: 1905
Former Name(s): None
Ground Address: Boothferry Park, Boothferry Road, Hull HU4 6EU
Phone Number: (01482) 351119

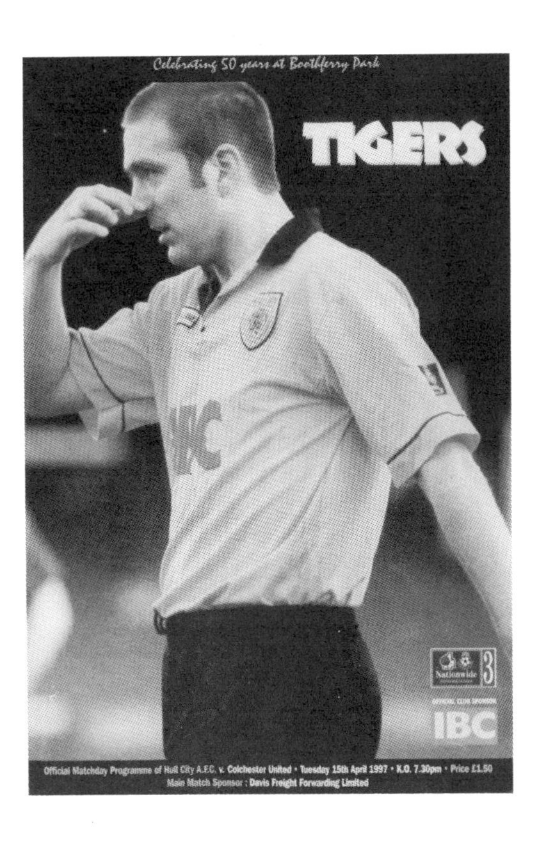

TECHNICAL INFORMATION

Size: 240mm x 163mm
Nº of Pages: 32
Price: £1.50
% Full Colour: 100%
% Adverts: 31.25%
% Content: 68.75%
Total Price per Page: 4.69p
Price per Page of Content: 6.82p
Printer: Strawberry CPS Limited
Editor: Robert Smith
Club Shop Phone: (01482) 328297

PROGRAMME MONTHLY REVIEW COMMENTS:

A much more subdued and more concentrated issue from HULL CITY, and it is all the better for that. The frenzied content and design of recent seasons has matured into a modern and attractive format, which disguises the comparative shortage of pages. Good level of reading, excellent spread of features, and attractive look – this is a splendid Third Division programme, and will surely be in contention for honours.

Ipswich Town FC

Founded: 1887 **Admitted to League**: 1938
Former Name(s): None
Ground Address: Portman Road, Ipswich IP1 2DA
Phone Number: (01473) 400500

TECHNICAL INFORMATION

Size: 221mm x 152mm
Nº of Pages: 36
Price: £1.50
% Full Colour: 100%
% Adverts: 22.22%
% Content: 77.78%
Total Price per Page: 4.17p
Price per Page of Content: 5.36p
Printer: Ancient House Press, Ipswich
Editor: Mike Noye
Club Shop Phone: (01473) 400500

PROGRAMME MONTHLY REVIEW COMMENTS:

A real shock from IPSWICH TOWN, who have dropped the large page size used for some decades, and returned to A5 size – against every trend in modern club programmes. The result is an attractive and colourful programme, but it compares poorly with the larger productions of the last 10 years. Advertising is more noticeable, and while a case could be put for the cover charge being justified by some interesting and informative features, the feeling is that the change of format is a retrograde step.

LEEDS UNITED FC

Founded: 1919 **Admitted to League**: 1920
Former Name(s): Formed after Leeds City FC wound up for irregular practices
Ground Address: Elland Road, Leeds LS11 0ES
Phone Number: (0113) 271-6037

TECHNICAL INFORMATION

Size: 239mm x 170mm
Nº of Pages: 52
Price: £1.70
% Full Colour: 100%
% Adverts: 30.77%
% Content: 69.23%
Total Price per Page: 3.27p
Price per Page of Content: 4.72p
Printer: Polar Print Group Limited
Editor: Mike Beddow, John Curtis
Club Shop Phone: (0113) 270-6844

PROGRAMME MONTHLY REVIEW COMMENTS:

This could be the year in which LEEDS UNITED lift the top programme award. If anything, they have improved the already impressive programme with more pages and resistance of temptation to charge more than £1.70. Design is extremely pleasant, being a clean, colourful look without being too overpowering. Reading matter is impressive, with a good variety of features. In short, an exquisite production.

LEICESTER CITY FC

Founded: 1884 **Admitted to League**: 1894
Former Name(s): Leicester Fosse FC (1884-1919)
Ground Address: City Stadium, Filbert Street, Leicester LE2 7FL
Phone Number: (0116) 291 5000

TECHNICAL INFORMATION

Size: 240mm x 170mm
Nº of Pages: 48
Price: £2.00
% Full Colour: 100%
% Adverts: 22.91%
% Content: 77.09%
Total Price per Page: 4.17p
Price per Page of Content: 5.26p
Printer: Printstream Limited
Editor: Paul Mace
Club Shop Phone: (0116) 291 5253

PROGRAMME MONTHLY REVIEW COMMENTS:

Another massive production from LEICESTER CITY, which has not dropped its phenomenally high standards of the last two seasons. No doubt the impetus of the return to the Premiership has sustained the enthusiasm of those responsible for this enormous undertaking. It is difficult to envisage how such a comprehensive match programme could be improved upon. A certain contender for honours.

LEYTON ORIENT FC

Founded: 1881 **Admitted to League**: 1905
Former Name(s): Glyn Cricket & Football Club (1881-86), Eagle FC (1886-88), Clapton Orient FC (1888-1946), Leyton Orient FC (1946-66), Orient FC (1966-87)
Ground Address: Leyton Stadium, Brisbane Road, Leyton, London E10 5NE
Phone Number: (0181) 539-2223

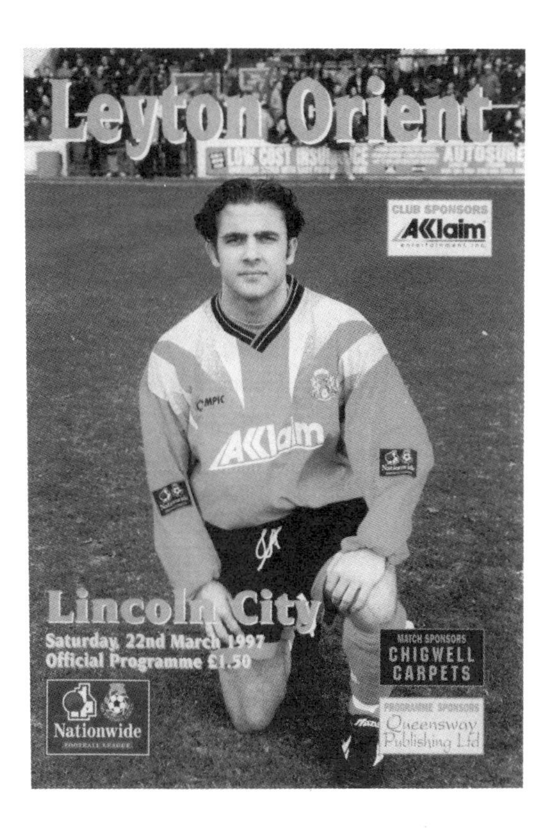

TECHNICAL INFORMATION

Size: 240mm x 167mm
Nº of Pages: 48
Price: £1.50
% Full Colour: 100%
% Adverts: 50.00%
% Content: 50.00%
Total Price per Page: 3.12p
Price per Page of Content: 6.25p
Printer: Queensway Publishing Limited, London
Editor: Trevor Davies & Tim Reder
Club Shop Phone: (0181) 539-2223

PROGRAMME MONTHLY REVIEW COMMENTS:

If there is a prize for the highest advertising content in a programme this season then LEYTON ORIENT will walk it – and presumably are unashamed in this. If that's what they want for their programme, then so be it, and it's a shame because the non-advertising pages (when you can find them) are good. Strong and attractive design, good reading, well presented – the trick is to find the content amongst the double-page advertising.

LINCOLN CITY FC

Founded: 1883 **Admitted to League**: 1892
Former Name(s): None
Ground Address: Sincil Bank, Lincoln LN5 8LD
Phone Number: (01522) 880011

TECHNICAL INFORMATION

Size: 244mm x 166mm
Nº of Pages: 32
Price: £1.50
% Full Colour: 40%
% Adverts: 31.25%
% Content: 68.75%
Total Price per Page: 4.69p
Price per Page of Content: 6.82p
Printer: Partners Press
Editor: None Credited
Club Shop Phone: (01522) 880011

PROGRAMME MONTHLY REVIEW COMMENTS:

LINCOLN CITY – 32 large pages £1.50, 10 advert pages continuing with the same format improved programme which has built upon the promise of the last few seasons. Design is "busy" and there is a good level of reading matter with some interesting features. Team lists no longer on the front cover and a little bit too heavy on the adverts and commercial matter but a reasonable programme nonetheless.

LIVERPOOL FC

Founded: 1892 **Admitted to League**: 1893
Former Name(s): None
Ground Address: Anfield Road, Liverpool L4 0TH
Phone Number: (0151) 263-2361

TECHNICAL INFORMATION

Size: 240mm x 170mm
Nº of Pages: 40
Price: £1.70
% Full Colour: 100%
% Adverts: 22.50%
% Content: 77.50%
Total Price per Page: 4.25p
Price per Page of Content: 5.48p
Printer: Rockcliff Printing Group, Liverpool
Editor: None credited
Club Shop Phone: (0151) 263-1760

PROGRAMME MONTHLY REVIEW COMMENTS:

LIVERPOOL have once again placed the emphasis on a pictorial coverage of club affairs, with comparatively brief features and limited reading for a 40 page programme. That said, there is full coverage of club affairs with an emphasis on imparting information, and good coverage of that day's fixture. Content wise, the programme should certainly be viewed as part of the range of club publications.

LUTON TOWN FC

Founded: 1885 **Admitted to League**: 1897
Former Name(s): Formed by amalgamation of Wanderers FC and Excelsior FC
Ground Address: Kenilworth Road Stadium, 1 Maple Road, Luton LU4 8AW
Phone Number: (01582) 411622

TECHNICAL INFORMATION

Size: 240mm x 170mm
Nº of Pages: 56
Price: £1.50
% Full Colour: 100%
% Adverts: 23.21%
% Content: 76.79%
Total Price per Page: 2.68p
Price per Page of Content: 3.49p
Printer: McLeod Warner
Editor: Simon Oxley
Club Shop Phone: (01582) 411622

PROGRAMME MONTHLY REVIEW COMMENTS:

Full marks to LUTON TOWN for maintaining their high standard of programme production despite suffering relegation last season. This is very much a modern issue, colourful with plenty of photographs and graphics. Take out the high advertising and commercial content, however, and there is a lack of substantial reading material. Allowances can be made, therefore, but this is a triumph of quantity over quality.

MANCHESTER CITY FC

Founded: 1887 **Admitted to League**: 1892
Former Name(s): Ardwick FC (1887-1894)
Ground Address: Maine Road, Moss Side, Manchester M14 7WN
Phone Number: (0161) 224-5000

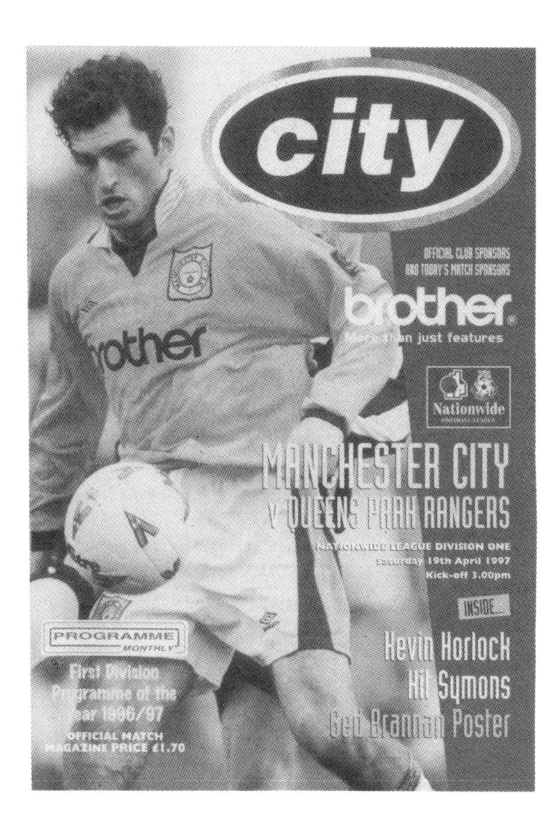

TECHNICAL INFORMATION

Size: 240mm x 170mm
Nº of Pages: 48
Price: £1.70
% Full Colour: 100%
% Adverts: 20.83%
% Content: 79.17%
Total Price per Page: 3.54p
Price per Page of Content: 4.47p
Printer: Polar Print Group
Editor: Mike Beddow
Club Shop Phone: (0161) 232-1111

PROGRAMME MONTHLY REVIEW COMMENTS:

MANCHESTER CITY may be toiling in the unaccustomed lower reaches of the First Division, but this is not reflected in their programme, which compares with the best in the Premiership. Exquisitely produced, masses of reading, well balanced features – the complete programme and certain contender for honours.

MANCHESTER UNITED FC

Founded: 1878 **Admitted to League**: 1892
Former Name(s): Newton Heath LYR FC (1878-1892), Newton Heath FC (1892-1902)
Ground Address: Old Trafford, Manchester M16 0RA
Phone Number: (0161) 872-1661

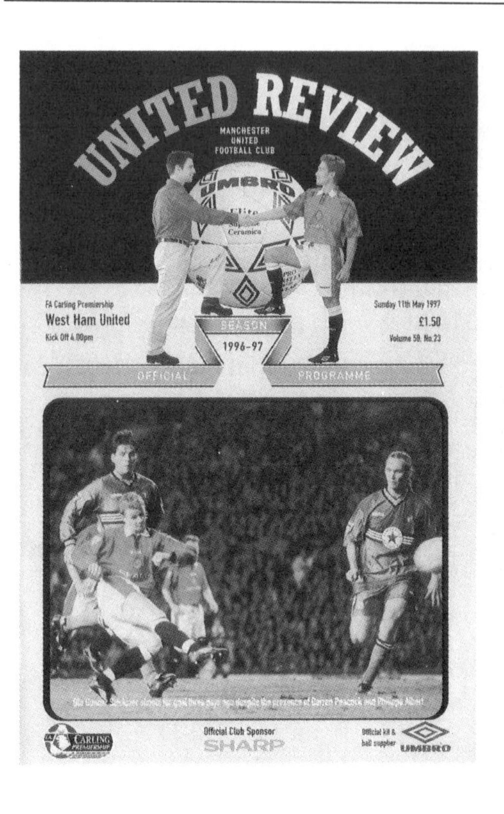

TECHNICAL INFORMATION

Size: 240mm x 170mm
Nº of Pages: 48
Price: £1.50
% Full Colour: 100%
% Adverts: 20.83%
% Content: 70.84%
Total Price per Page: 3.12p
Price per Page of Content: 3.94p
Printer: Trafford Press
Editor: Cliff Butler
Club Shop Phone: (0161) 872-3398

PROGRAMME MONTHLY REVIEW COMMENTS:

The MANCHESTER UNITED programme is a truly gorgeous production, with the very highest standard of design, print and paper. It is too easy to unfavourably compare this issue with the low-advert, low- cover price issues of some years ago, but that would not take into account the quality of features, and high level of content and reading of this modern issue. "United Review" could well be back in serious contention for honours. Design & layout, The Wolff Evans Partnership.

Mansfield Town FC

Founded: 1891 **Admitted to League**: 1931
Former Name(s): Mansfield Wesleyans FC (1891-1905)
Ground Address: Field Mill Ground, Quarry Lane, Mansfield, Notts.
Phone Number: (01623) 23567

TECHNICAL INFORMATION

Size: 245mm x 165mm
Nº of Pages: 32
Price: £1.30
% Full Colour: 28%
% Adverts: 28.12%
% Content: 71.88%
Total Price per Page: 4.06p
Price per Page of Content: 5.65p
Printer: Partners Press, Newark
Editor: None credited
Club Shop Phone: (01623) 658070

PROGRAMME MONTHLY REVIEW COMMENTS:

MANSFIELD TOWN continue to infuriate by their mixture of good and disappointing. Design and presentation is pleasant and bright, despite the comparative lack of full colour. There is a reasonable level of reading matter, but the programme lacks a cohesive editorial, and there is a measure of space filling. Unchanging cover design does not help, Although the £1.30 price tag does.

MIDDLESBROUGH FC

Founded: 1876 **Admitted to League**: 1899
Former Name(s): None
Ground Address: Cellnet Riverside Stadium, Middlesbrough, Cleveland TS6 3RS
Phone Number: (01642) 877700

TECHNICAL INFORMATION

Size: 235mm x 165mm
Nº of Pages: 48
Price: £1.50
% Full Colour: 100%
% Adverts: 35.42%
% Content: 64.58%
Total Price per Page: 3.12p
Price per Page of Content: 4.84p
Printer: Hillprint
Editor: Adrian Bevington
Club Shop Phone: (01643) 877720

PROGRAMME MONTHLY REVIEW COMMENTS:

A real problem for MIDDLESBROUGH this season – how do you follow the last two seasons' stunning programmes? Their solution is to completely revamp the issue. Paper, colour and design is outstanding, but sometimes this is at the expense of words and there is the occasional hint of large type size. A beautiful programme, and outstanding value for money – its only problem being the comparison with last season's excellent, and very different, issue.

MILLWALL FC

Founded: 1885 **Admitted to League**: 1920
Former Name(s): Millwall Rovers FC, Millwall Athletic FC
Ground Address: The Den, Zampa Rd, London SE16 3LN
Phone Number: (0171) 232-1222

TECHNICAL INFORMATION

Size: 240mm x 168mm
Nº of Pages: 40
Price: £1.70
% Full Colour: 100%
% Adverts: 22.5%
% Content: 77.5%
Total Price per Page: 4.25p
Price per Page of Content: 5.48p
Printer: Sports & Leisure Print, Mitcham
Editor: Deano Standing
Club Shop Phone: (0171) 231-9845

PROGRAMME MONTHLY REVIEW COMMENTS:

There must be something in the South London air that encourages bold primary colours in its programmes, for MILLWALL have a bright and brash issue similar to Wimbledon's. It's pretty good, too, with plenty of features, good reading matter and a nice balance to content. Some of the text size is of the spacefilling variety – other articles are set in tiny type. Millwall have always priced at the top end of the spectrum, but this is good value for money.

NEWCASTLE UNITED FC

Founded: 1882 **Admitted to League**: 1893

Former Name(s): Newcastle East End FC (1882-1892); became United when amalgamated with Newcastle West End FC

Ground Address: St. James Park, Newcastle-upon-Tyne NE1 4ST

Phone Number: (0191) 201-8400

TECHNICAL INFORMATION

Size: 240mm x 168mm

Nº of Pages: 48

Price: £1.50

% Full Colour: 100%

% Adverts: 25%

% Content: 75%

Total Price per Page: 3.12p

Price per Page of Content: 4.17p

Printer: Mayflower Printers

Editor: Tony Hardisty

Club Shop Phone: (0191) 201-8401

PROGRAMME MONTHLY REVIEW COMMENTS:

A highly coloured and strongly design match programme which reflects the stature of NEWCASTLE UNITED. The emphasis is very much on pictorial coverage and small bite-sized features. Authoriative on club affairs, and deserving of great praise in this considering the competing media calls on the club. To the delight of many, coverage of other sports in which the club is involved has gone. Up with the best in its Division, and a real contender for honours.

NORTHAMPTON TOWN FC

Founded: 1897 **Admitted to League**: 1920
Former Name(s): None
Ground Address: Sixfields Stadium, Upton Way, Northampton NN5 4EG
Phone Number: (01604) 757773

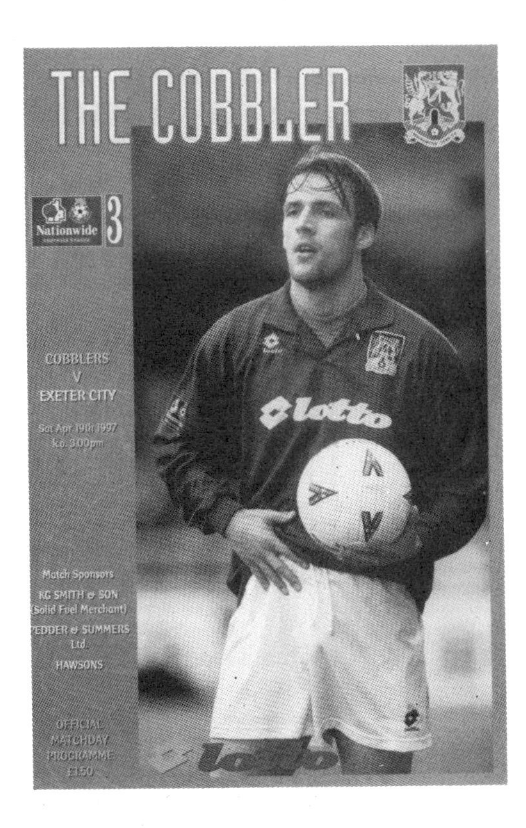

TECHNICAL INFORMATION

Size: 240mm x 159mm
Nº of Pages: 48
Price: £1.50
% Full Colour: 40%
% Adverts: 52.08%
% Content: 47.92%
Total Price per Page: 3.12p
Price per Page of Content: 6.52p
Printer: Avalon Print, Northampton
Editor: Mike Berry
Club Shop Phone: (01604) 757773

PROGRAMME MONTHLY REVIEW COMMENTS:

Plenty of pages – plenty of adverts, although there is a high reading level with some good, solid features in the NORTHAMPTON TOWN programme. Given its very high level of advertising and commercial coverage, they're pushing it a bit at £1.50. Design is quite ordinary, leading to an unfortunately dull look to the spot colour pages (which comprise two thirds of the programme). The fans will like this issue, though, albeit they are paying top price.

NORWICH CITY FC

Founded: 1902 **Admitted to League**: 1920

Former Name(s): None

Ground Address: Carrow Road, Norwich NR1 1JE

Phone Number: (01603) 760760

TECHNICAL INFORMATION

Size: 240mm x 164mm

Nº of Pages: 32

Price: £1.50

% Full Colour: 100%

% Adverts: 21.87%

% Content: 78.13%

Total Price per Page: 4.69p

Price per Page of Content: 6.00

Printer: Breckland Print Limited, Attleborough

Editor: Kevan Platt

Club Shop Phone: (01603) 761125

PROGRAMME MONTHLY REVIEW COMMENTS:

There has been a radical re-design of the NORWICH CITY programme, and it must be classed a success. Fewer pages, but better use of space and more economy of design has meant little-or-no loss of content, and arguably a more attractive final product. Type size must be the smallest in the country, and while the first half of the programme concentrates on some substantial articles and features, the second half has a "busier" look with plenty of bite-sized features. Extremely attractive, good value for money, and a testament to the hard work of the editor and production team.

NOTTINGHAM FOREST FC

Founded: 1865 **Admitted to League**: 1892
Former Name(s): None
Ground Address: City Ground, Nottingham NG2 5FJ
Phone Number: (0115) 952-6000

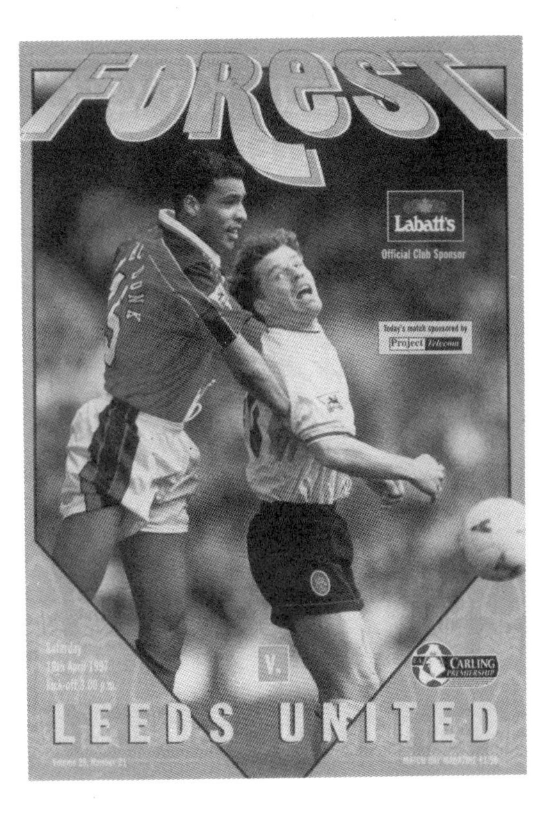

TECHNICAL INFORMATION

Size: 239mm x 168mm
Nº of Pages: 40
Price: £1.50
% Full Colour: 100%
% Adverts: 25%
% Content: 75%
Total Price per Page: 3.75p
Price per Page of Content: 5.00p
Printer: Temple Printing
Editor: Lawson & Bowles
Club Shop Phone: (0115) 952-6026

PROGRAMME MONTHLY REVIEW COMMENTS:

Extremely attractive issue from NOTTINGHAM FOREST, and it would appear from this that the difficult transition from the highly distinctive letter-press issue of the black, to a programme of modern standards, has been completed. Good level of reading, although the second half is somewhat advertising-laden, but this is a very nice issue, good value and can compare with anything in the Premiership.

NOTTS COUNTY FC

Founded: 1862 **Admitted to League**: 1888
Former Name(s): None
Ground Address: Meadow Lane, Nottingham NG2 3HJ
Phone Number: (0115) 952-9000

TECHNICAL INFORMATION

Size: 239mm x 167mm
Nº of Pages: 32
Price: £1.50
% Full Colour: 50%
% Adverts: 37.5%
% Content: 62.5%
Total Price per Page: 4.69p
Price per Page of Content: 7.50p
Printer: DESA Limited
Editor: Terry Bowles
Club Shop Phone: (0115) 952-9000

PROGRAMME MONTHLY REVIEW COMMENTS:

This season sees a more restrained, condensed NOTTS COUNTY programme, and it is all the better for that. Gone are the days of many pages and many more adverts, and this is a tight, well balanced production. Excellent range of articles, plenty to read with the emphasis placed on content rather than cover-to-cover colour. Design and presentation is, nonetheless, well up to standard.

OLDHAM ATHLETIC FC

Founded: 1895 **Admitted to League**: 1907
Former Name(s): Pine Villa FC (1895-1899)
Ground Address: Boundary Park, Oldham OL1 2PA
Phone Number: (0161) 624-4972

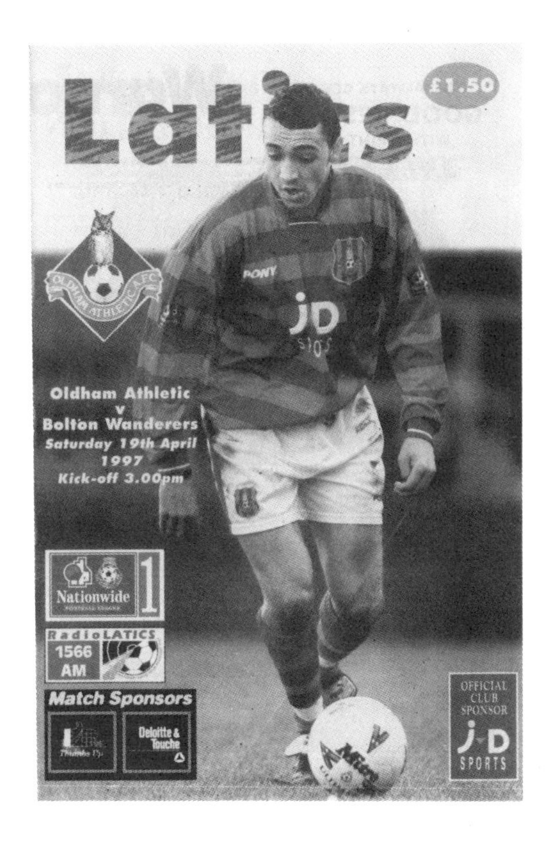

TECHNICAL INFORMATION

Size: 244mm x 165mm
Nº of Pages: 40
Price: £1.50
% Full Colour: 100%
% Adverts: 32.5%
% Content: 67.5%
Total Price per Page: 3.75p
Price per Page of Content: 5.56p
Printer: Windmill Print and Design
Editor: A. Hardy
Club Shop Phone: (0161) 652-0966

PROGRAMME MONTHLY REVIEW COMMENTS:

OLDHAM ATHLETIC is a club not over-burdened by paying spectators and the Latics use their hefty investment in a prestigious programme to good effect, packing in plenty of club information. If anything is in short supply, it is probably some features, although the two major items that are included are readable and entertaining.

OXFORD UNITED FC

Founded: 1893 **Admitted to League**: 1962
Former Name(s): Headington United FC (1893-1960)
Ground Address: Manor Ground, London Road, Headington, Oxford OX3 7RS
Phone Number: (01865) 761503

TECHNICAL INFORMATION

Size: 239mm x 168mm
Nº of Pages: 32
Price: £1.50
% Full Colour: 25%
% Adverts: 9.37%
% Content: 90.63%
Total Price per Page: 4.69p
Price per Page of Content: 5.17p
Printer: Queensway Publishing, London
Editor: Ian Davies
Club Shop Phone: (01865) 761503

PROGRAMME MONTHLY REVIEW COMMENTS:

Don't be misled by the comparative lack of pages in the OXFORD UNITED programme – this is more than compensated by a miniscule advertising/commerical coverage, and the superb quality of the remainder of the pages. This is an example of a club making full use of the services of a top-line printer, and the result is a programme that would not be out of place in the Premiership. Plenty to read, attractively and imaginitively presented, giving full coverage of current club affairs. A splendid programme that is sure to be appreciated by supporters.

PETERBOROUGH UNITED FC

Founded: 1923 **Admitted to League**: 1960
Former Name(s): Peterborough & Fletton United FC (1923-1934)
Ground Address: London Road, Peterborough, Cambs. PE2 8AZ
Phone Number: (01733) 63947

TECHNICAL INFORMATION

Size: 244mm x 160mm
Nº of Pages: 32
Price: £1.50
% Full Colour: 100%
% Adverts: 37.50%
% Content: 62.50%
Total Price per Page: 4.69p
Price per Page of Content: 6.00p
Printer: Windmill Printing
Editor: Russell Plummer
Club Shop Phone: (01733) 69760

PROGRAMME MONTHLY REVIEW COMMENTS:

PETERBOROUGH UNITED have extended full colour to all pages, and have produced a bright and breezy production with a good-looking economy of design. They have also increased the cover price to the now almost universal benchmark of £1.50. What they haven't done is increase pages or reduce advertising/commercial items. A nice looking programme, but short on content for the price.

Plymouth Argyle FC

Founded: 1886 **Admitted to League**: 1920
Former Name(s): Argyle FC (1886-1903)
Ground Address: Home Park, Plymouth PL2 3DQ
Phone Number: (01752) 562561

TECHNICAL INFORMATION

Size: 238mm x 167mm
Nº of Pages: 48
Price: £1.50
% Full Colour: 80%
% Adverts: 29.17%
% Content: 70.83%
Total Price per Page: 3.12p
Price per Page of Content: 4.41p
Printer: Kingfisher Print & Design, Dartington
Editor: Steve Hill
Club Shop Phone: (01752) 558292

PROGRAMME MONTHLY REVIEW COMMENTS:

There can be no higher accolade than saying that PLYMOUTH ARGYLE would be in contention for honours in the Premiership. Any changes from last season's marvellous award winner are for the better. Absolutely packed with information, features and photographs, and as always with a Kingfisher programme, those pages that are not full colour are cleverly designed with good use of spot colour. Quite superb.

PORTSMOUTH FC

Founded: 1898 **Admitted to League**: 1920

Former Name(s): None

Ground Address: Fratton Park, 57 Frogmore Road, Portsmouth, Hants. PO4 8RA

Phone Number: (01705) 731204

TECHNICAL INFORMATION

Size: 240mm x 170mm

Nº of Pages: 32

Price: £1.50

% Full Colour: 100%

% Adverts: 29.69%

% Content: 70.31%

Total Price per Page: 4.68p

Price per Page of Content: 6.67p

Printer: Bishops Printers Limited, Portsmouth

Editor: Julie Baker

Club Shop Phone: (01705) 738358

PROGRAMME MONTHLY REVIEW COMMENTS:

Very bright and quite breezy – a really colourful issue from PORTSMOUTH which performs the basics well. Good reading material but there is little room for anything other than standard features, and it is disappointing in such a (comparatively) slim volume to find some syndicated features. Not bad at all, but not in the same class as the top rate Pompey issues of old.

Port Vale FC

Founded: 1876 **Admitted to League**: 1892
Former Name(s): Burslem Port Vale FC (1876-1913)
Ground Address: Vale Park, Burslem, Stoke-on-Trent ST6 1AW
Phone Number: (01782) 814134

TECHNICAL INFORMATION

Size: 240mm x 166mm
Nº of Pages: 40
Price: £1.50
% Full Colour: 100%
% Adverts: 30%
% Content: 70%
Total Price per Page: 3.75p
Price per Page of Content: 5.36p
Printer: Colourplan Design & Print, St. Helens
Editor: Chris Harper
Club Shop Phone: (01782) 833545

PROGRAMME MONTHLY REVIEW COMMENTS:

PORT VALE have disappointed a little this season, as there programme shows a fall in standards from last year. Print quality and design is well up to standard, although not quite as innovative as last season, but there is the definite air of "space filling" about the production, starting with much of page three given over to a list of contents. Text is large, there are plenty of photographs and no shortage of advertisement/commercial coverage. Looks good, but content is lacking.

Preston North End FC

Founded: 1881 **Admitted to League**: 1888

Former Name(s): None

Ground Address: Deepdale, Preston PR1 6RU

Phone Number: (01772) 902000

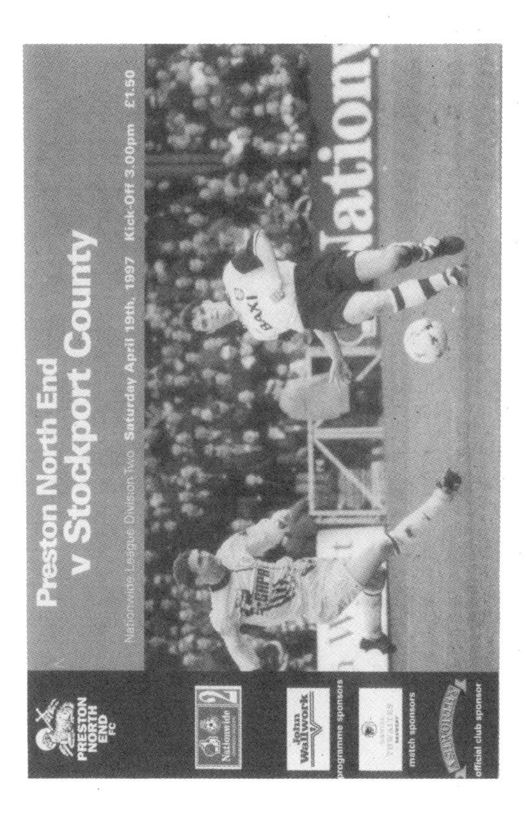

TECHNICAL INFORMATION

Size: 158mm x 237mm

Nº of Pages: 40

Price: £1.50

% Full Colour: 100%

% Adverts: 22.5%

% Content: 77.5%

Total Price per Page: 3.75p

Price per Page of Content: 4.69p

Printer: Mercer Print, Accrington

Editor: Steve Wilkinson

Club Shop Phone: (01772) 902040

PROGRAMME MONTHLY REVIEW COMMENTS:

A very different production from PRESTON NORTH END, with staple along the short side and a simple, but attractive, page design. Refreshingly different, with plenty to read and a good range of features. There is room for some improvement, as the design does eat up space, and the second half in particular is prone to commercial/advertising coverage, but this is a fine production.

QUEEN'S PARK RANGERS FC

Founded: 1882 **Admitted to League**: 1920
Former Name(s): Formed by amalgamation of St. Jude's & Christchurch Rangers FC
Ground Address: Rangers Stadium, South Africa Road, London W12 7PA
Phone Number: (0181) 743-0262

TECHNICAL INFORMATION

Size: 245mm x 167mm
Nº of Pages: 36
Price: £1.50
% Full Colour: 100%
% Adverts: 11.11%
% Content: 88.89%
Total Price per Page: 4.16p
Price per Page of Content: 4.55p
Printer: None Credited
Editor: None Credited
Club Shop Phone: (0181) 749-6862

PROGRAMME MONTHLY REVIEW COMMENTS:

Gone is the magazine style of last seasons at QUEEN'S PARK RANGERS, and in its place a thoroughly comprehensive programme with an astonishingly low advertising threshold. Design is very simple and understated, which perhaps exposes a little bit of large-print-syndrome, but there are acres of reading material, resulting in a thoroughly informative issue which is excellent value for money.

READING FC

Founded: 1871 **Admitted to League**: 1920
Former Name(s): Amalgamated with Hornets FC (1877) and Earley FC (1889)
Ground Address: Elm Park, Norfolk Road, Reading RG3 2EF
Phone Number: (01189) 507878

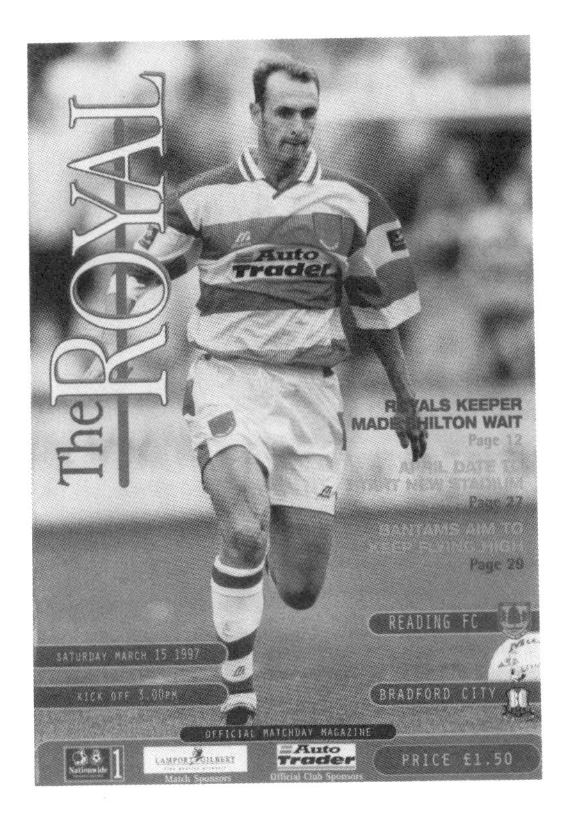

TECHNICAL INFORMATION

Size: 240mm x 169mm
Nº of Pages: 48
Price: £1.50
% Full Colour: 100%
% Adverts: 37.5%
% Content: 62.5%
Total Price per Page: 3.12p
Price per Page of Content: 5.00p
Printer: Morganprint Limited, Charlton
Editor: Maurice O'Brien
Club Shop Phone: (01189) 507878

PROGRAMME MONTHLY REVIEW COMMENTS:

The READING programme this season is quite stunning, beautifully produced in full colour on top quality paper. Design and print is of the highest quality, with a rare feat being achieved – there is an uncluttered and spacious look to the programme, with no diminution in quantity of text. Features are first class and of a substantial nature, with full coverage of club affairs. It is no exaggeration to say that this is one of the very best in the First Division.

ROCHDALE FC

Founded: 1907 **Admitted to League**: 1921
Former Name(s): Rochdale Town FC
Ground Address: Willbutts Lane, Spotland, Rochdale OL11 5DS
Phone Number: (01706) 44648

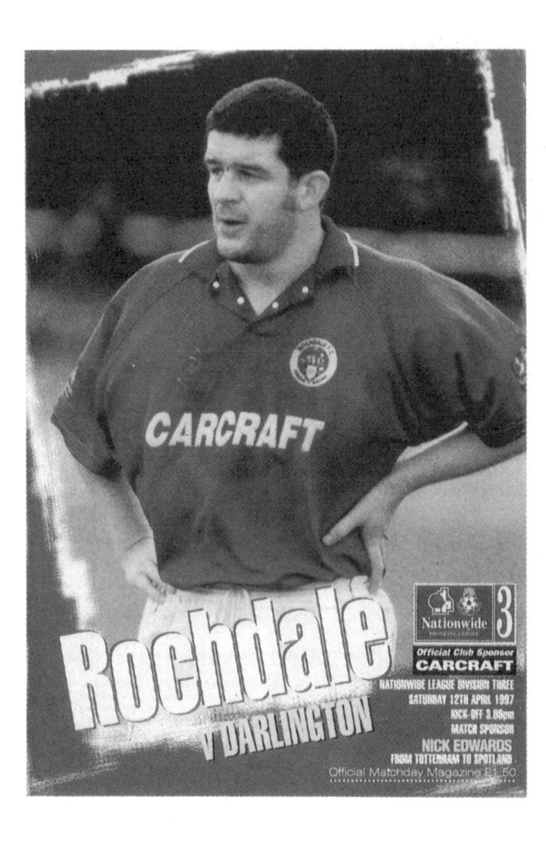

TECHNICAL INFORMATION

Size: 240mm x 167mm
Nº of Pages: 32
Price: £1.50
% Full Colour: 100%
% Adverts: 28.12%
% Content: 71.88%
Total Price per Page: 4.68p
Price per Page of Content: 6.52p
Printer: Colourplan
Editor: Stephen Walmsley
Club Shop Phone: (01706) 47521

PROGRAMME MONTHLY REVIEW COMMENTS:

Another pleasant issue from ROCHDALE, with a good blend of attractive spot blue design and full colour pages. There are some meaty features which, combined with the attractive presentation and modern format, make for a most satisfactory production.

ROTHERHAM UNITED FC

Founded: 1884 **Admitted to League**: 1920
Former Name(s): Thornhill United FC (1884-1905), Rotherham County FC (1905-1925)
Ground Address: Millmoor Ground, Rotherham S60 1HR
Phone Number: (01709) 512434

TECHNICAL INFORMATION

Size: 223mm x 158mm
Nº of Pages: 44
Price: £1.50
% Full Colour: 100%
% Adverts: 31.82%
% Content: 68.28%
Total Price per Page: 3.41p
Price per Page of Content: 5.00p
Printer: None credited
Editor: D. Nicholls and G.A. Somerton
Club Shop Phone: (01709) 512760

PROGRAMME MONTHLY REVIEW COMMENTS:

The usual enigma from ROTHERHAM UNITED – with a mixture of the very good, and the missed opportunity. Presentation is colourful and bright, and there is a wide and varied range of features. Advertising and commercial coverage overwhelms everything else in this attractive issue, however, and the club's stall has been set out in this respect.

SCARBOROUGH FC

Founded: 1879 **Admitted to League**: 1987
Former Name(s): None
Ground Address: McCain Stadium, Seamer Road, Scarborough, North Yorkshire, YO12 4HF
Phone Number: (01723) 375094

TECHNICAL INFORMATION

Size: 240mm x 165mm
Nº of Pages: 36
Price: £1.50
% Full Colour: 22%
% Adverts: 47.22%
% Content: 52.78%
Total Price per Page: 4.17p
Price per Page of Content: 7.89p
Printer: HPE Print, Pickering
Editor: E. Pickup
Club Shop Phone: (01723) 375094

PROGRAMME MONTHLY REVIEW COMMENTS:

Improved issue from SCARBOROUGH, and while clearly no world-beater, there is refreshing acknowledgement of this in its cover price. Bright and pleasant design and format, with a reasonable spread of features. Most importantly, there has been a significant improvement from previous seasons, and there is hope (and scope) for further improvements in future.

SCUNTHORPE UNITED FC

Founded: 1899 **Admitted to League**: 1950
Former Name(s): Scunthorpe & Lindsey United (1899-1912)
Ground Address: Glanford Park, Doncaster Road, Scunthorpe DN15 8TD
Phone Number: (01724) 848077

TECHNICAL INFORMATION

Size: 245mm x 165mm
№ of Pages: 32
Price: £1.50
% Full Colour: 29%
% Adverts: 20.31%
% Content: 79.69%
Total Price per Page: 4.69p
Price per Page of Content: 5.88p
Printer: Partners Press
Editor: John Curtis and Andy Skeels
Club Shop Phone: (01724) 848077

PROGRAMME MONTHLY REVIEW COMMENTS:

The SCUNTHORPE UNITED programme was much improved last season and that has been sustained into the new season. Design is unpretentious, and the non colour pages are in stark black and white, but the programme is pleasing to the eye and the features have impact with bold presentation. Plenty to read, with a good mix of features – a first class programme.

Sheffield United FC

Founded: 1889 **Admitted to League**: 1892
Former Name(s): None
Ground Address: Bramall Lane, Sheffield S2 4SU
Phone Number: (0114) 221-5757

TECHNICAL INFORMATION

Size: 241mm x 168mm
Nº of Pages: 40
Price: £1.50
% Full Colour: 100%
% Adverts: 32.5%
% Content: 67.5%
Total Price per Page: 3.75p
Price per Page of Content: 5.56p
Printer: Polar Print Group, Leicester
Editor: Andy Pack
Club Shop Phone: (0114) 221-3129

PROGRAMME MONTHLY REVIEW COMMENTS:

One opens the SHEFFIELD UNITED programme each season expecting a first class, professional, modern and value-for-money production, and this season is no exception. Beautifully produced, colourful, there is plenty to read and a full range of club features, with additional columns on a wider footballing perspective. One of the best in its Division, and a programme that would certainly not be out of place in the Premiership.

SHEFFIELD WEDNESDAY FC

Founded: 1867 **Admitted to League**: 1892
Former Name(s): The Wednesday FC
Ground Address: Hillsborough, Sheffield S6 1SW
Phone Number: (0114) 221-2121

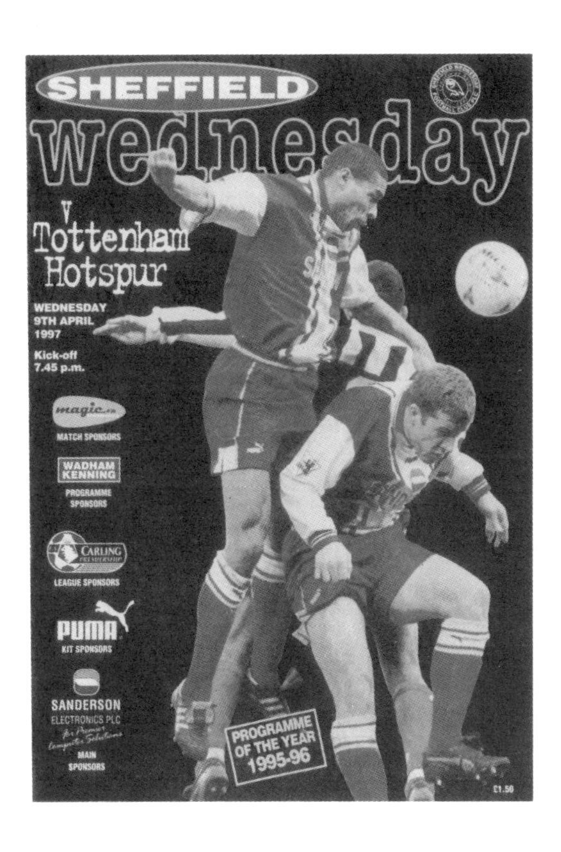

TECHNICAL INFORMATION

Size: 241mm x 169mm
Nº of Pages: 46
Price: £1.50
% Full Colour: 100%
% Adverts: 26.08%
% Content: 73.92%
Total Price per Page: 3.26p
Price per Page of Content: 4.41p
Printer: J.W. Northend Limited, Sheffield
Editor: Roger Oldfield
Club Shop Phone: (0114) 221-2345

PROGRAMME MONTHLY REVIEW COMMENTS:

In terms of quality of presentation SHEFFIELD WEDNESDAY would be hard to beat any season, with their top class colour and print, thick glossy paper and part-laminated covers. Content is up to its usual high and informative standard, although in common with many of its type, the concentration on pictorial coverage and design often subordinates text.

SHREWSBURY TOWN FC

Founded: 1886 **Admitted to League**: 1950
Former Name(s): None
Ground Address: Gay Meadow, Shrewsbury SY2 6AB
Phone Number: (01743) 360111

TECHNICAL INFORMATION

Size: 226mm x 155mm
Nº of Pages: 32
Price: £1.40
% Full Colour: 12.5%
% Adverts: 25%
% Content: 75%
Total Price per Page: 4.38p
Price per Page of Content: 5.83p
Printer: Pemandos A&M
Editor: Don Stanton
Club Shop Phone: (01743) 356316

PROGRAMME MONTHLY REVIEW COMMENTS:

One can just predict how the SHREWSBURY TOWN programme will look every season, and the club – and its supporters – seem content with Don Stanton's production style. There is plenty to read, all of it entertaining and informative, and there is exhaustive coverage of club affairs. While the design and presentation cannot, by any stretch of the imagination, be compared with the majority of modern League club programmes, the distinctive style has a certain charm and attraction of its own. Refreshingly different, and in terms of content undoubted value for money.

SOUTHAMPTON FC

Founded: 1885 **Admitted to League**: 1920
Former Name(s): Southampton St. Mary's YMCA FC (1885-1897)
Ground Address: The Dell, Milton Road, Southampton SO9 4XX
Phone Number: (01703) 220505

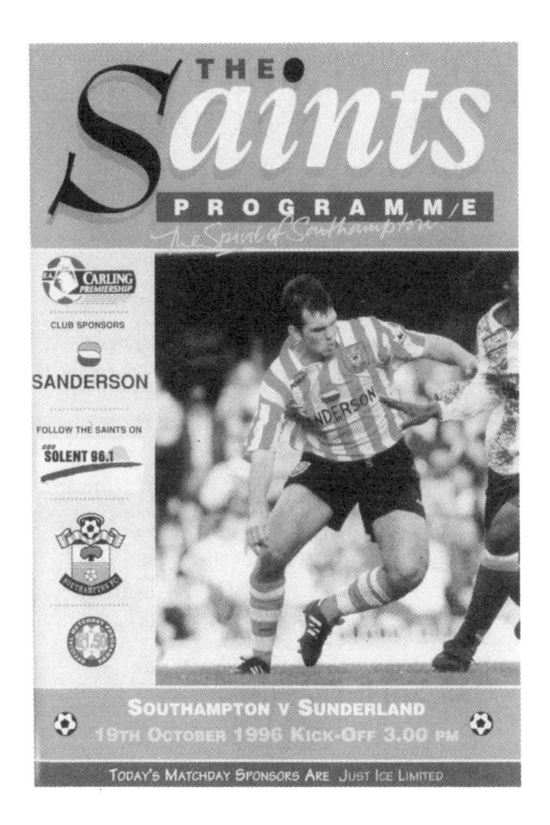

TECHNICAL INFORMATION

Size: 240mm x 163mm
Nº of Pages: 48
Price: £1.50
% Full Colour: 100%
% Adverts: 22.92%
% Content: 77.08%
Total Price per Page: 3.12p
Price per Page of Content: 4.05p
Printer: Cedar Press
Editor: None credited
Club Shop Phone: (01703) 236400

PROGRAMME MONTHLY REVIEW COMMENTS:

Superb looking programme from SOUTHAMPTON, with top quality print, paper and design – in fact it is arguably the best looking issue in England this season. Content has improved in quantity from last season, with less obvious space-filling, although 'the emphasis remains on photographs and graphics. There are a few substantial features to balance the snippets of club information, in this well-rounded production.

Southend United FC

Founded: 1906 **Admitted to League**: 1920
Former Name(s): Southend Athletic FC
Ground Address: Roots Hall Ground, Victoria Avenue, Southend-on-Sea SS2 6NQ
Phone Number: (01702) 304050

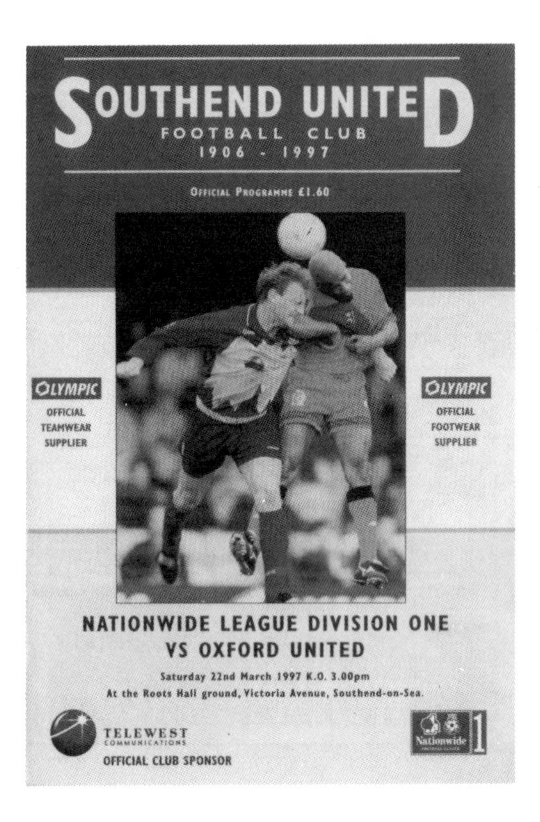

TECHNICAL INFORMATION

Size: 239mm x 165mm
Nº of Pages: 48
Price: £1.60
% Full Colour: 100%
% Adverts: 41.67%
% Content: 58.33%
Total Price per Page: 3.33p
Price per Page of Content: 5.71p
Printer: Progressive Printing (UK) Limited
Editor: K. O'Donnell
Club Shop Phone: (01702) 601351

PROGRAMME MONTHLY REVIEW COMMENTS:

SOUTHEND UNITED are still underachieving with their large programmme. The basis for an excellent issue is there - plenty of pages, good quality and print and a good range of interesting features, but advertising is heaving and pervades most pages; type-faces are large and there is an overall impression of space-filling. Some of the pages have an unnecessary dull look as a consequence. Less pages and a more concentrated effort would have resulted in a better product – but then again, there wouldn't have been the same amount of advertising.

STOCKPORT COUNTY FC

Founded: 1883 **Admitted to League**: 1900
Former Name(s): Heaton Norris Rovers FC, Heaton Norris FC
Ground Address: Edgeley Park, Hardcastle Road, Edgeley, Stockport SK3 9DD
Phone Number: (0161) 286-8888

TECHNICAL INFORMATION

Size: 240mm x 167mm
Nº of Pages: 56
Price: £1.50
% Full Colour: 100%
% Adverts: 42.86%
% Content: 57.14%
Total Price per Page: 2.67p
Price per Page of Content: 4.17p
Printer: Colourplan
Editor: None Credited
Club Shop Phone: (0161) 286-8899

PROGRAMME MONTHLY REVIEW COMMENTS:

How do they do it? Every season the massive STOCKPORT COUNTY issue seems to improve, illustrating to all clubs out of the top flight what can be achieved with a will, and plenty of hard work. There is a less frenetic look to the programme's design, although this is still a "hits you between the eyes" programme. In terms of content, it just about has everything, and is now an overall more rounded and polished production, while remaining superb value for money. Needless to say, this is a contender for honours.

STOKE CITY FC

Founded: 1863 **Admitted to League**: 1888
Former Name(s): Stoke FC
Ground Address: Britannia Stadium, Stoke-on-Trent, Staffs.
Phone Number: (01782) 252525

TECHNICAL INFORMATION

Size: 244mm x 165mm
№ of Pages: 48
Price: £1.50
% Full Colour: 100%
% Adverts: 33.33%
% Content: 66.67%
Total Price per Page: 3.12p
Price per Page of Content: 4.69p
Printer: None Credited
Editor: None Credited
Club Shop Phone: (01782) 747078

PROGRAMME MONTHLY REVIEW COMMENTS:

STOKE CITY have, in recent years, provided a good read and invariably a substantial and colourful programme. This season's programme is mildly disappointing in the noticeable advertising and commercial content. That said. there are some good, club-orientated features with supporters having their say, although not to the extent of last season's excellent coverage. Price is reasonable for a 48 page programme.

SUNDERLAND AFC

Founded: 1879 **Admitted to League**: 1890

Former Name(s): Sunderland and District Teachers FC

Ground Address: New Stadium, Monkwearmouth, Co. Durham (**Note**: At time of publication new stadium name was unknown)

Phone Number: (0191) 514-0332

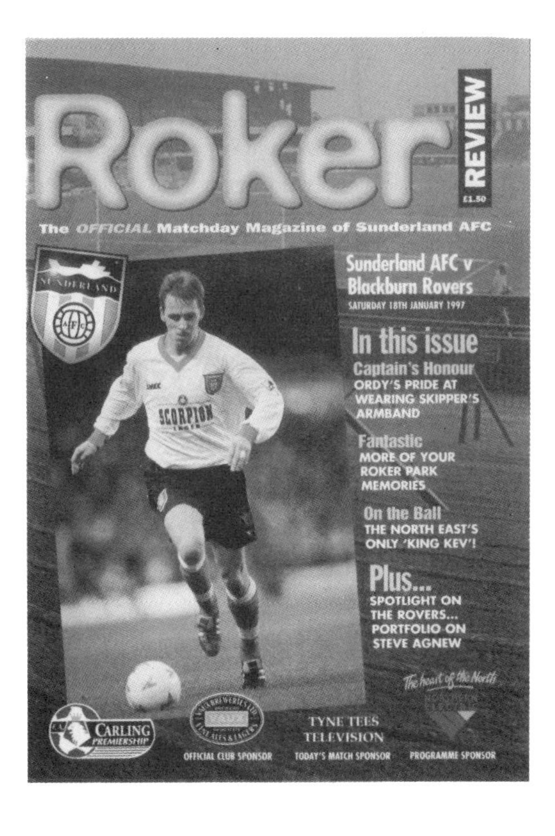

TECHNICAL INFORMATION

Size: 240mm x 170mm

Nº of Pages: 48

Price: £1.50

% Full Colour: 100%

% Adverts: 27.77%

% Content: 72.23%

Total Price per Page: 3.12p

Price per Page of Content: 5.76p

Printer: Polar Print

Editor: Rob Mason

Club Shop Phone: (0191) 385-2778

PROGRAMME MONTHLY REVIEW COMMENTS:

A lovely big-time programme from the resurgent SUNDERLAND, with rich colouration and design and excellent range and depth of features. Full value for its cover price, this is up with the best in the Premiership, and completes the transformation of the always-promising, but invariably underachieving, Sunderland programmes of recent years.

SWANSEA CITY FC

Founded: 1900 **Admitted to League**: 1920
Former Name(s): Swansea Town FC (1900-1970)
Ground Address: Vetch Field, Swansea SA1 3SU
Phone Number: (01792) 474114

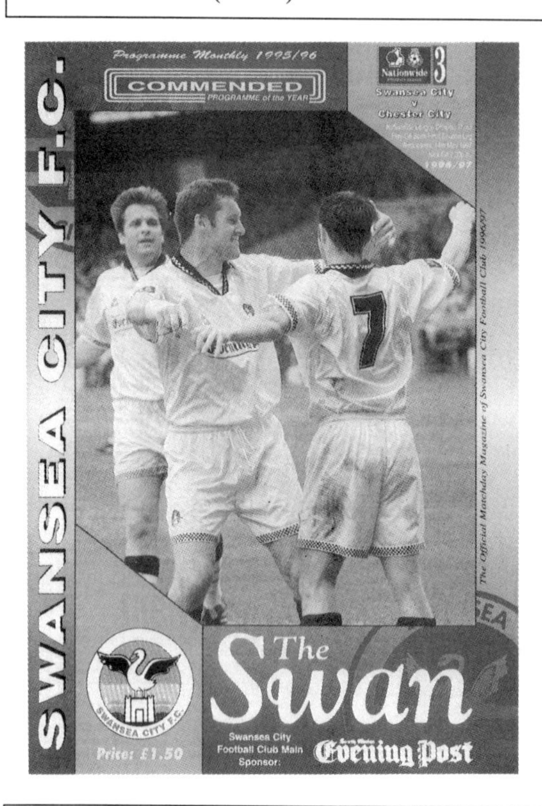

TECHNICAL INFORMATION

Size: 235mm x 165mm
Nº of Pages: 32
Price: £1.50
% Full Colour: 100%
% Adverts: 31.25%
% Content: 68.75%
Total Price per Page: 4.69p
Price per Page of Content: 5.90p
Printer: PRS Associates
Editor: Reg Pike
Club Shop Phone: (01792) 462584

PROGRAMME MONTHLY REVIEW COMMENTS:

The SWANSEA CITY programme continues to make progress, with an extremely bright and professional production deflecting some attention from a lack of major features. The programme "does the basics" very well, and information is to the fore. Those features (or historical items, current playing matters etc) which are included are too brief, however. It is always difficult and often unfair to criticise Third Division clubs for what their programmes lack, given the constraints of low attendances, while this is as good as Swansea have produced in the past, it has to be admitted that others in their Division do it better.

SWINDON TOWN FC

Founded: 1881 **Admitted to League**: 1920

Former Name(s): None

Ground Address: Country Ground, County Road, Swindon SN1 2ED

Phone Number: (01793) 430430

TECHNICAL INFORMATION

Size: 240mm x 164mm

Nº of Pages: 48

Price: £1.80

% Full Colour: 100%

% Adverts: 25%

% Content: 75%

Total Price per Page: 3.75p

Price per Page of Content: 5.00p

Printer: PIA Advertising & Marketing

Editor: Jason Harris

Club Shop Phone: (01793) 423030

PROGRAMME MONTHLY REVIEW COMMENTS:

The SWINDON TOWN programme is exquisitely produced, with stunning colour and imaginitive design and presentation. Features are "bite sized" in the modern idiom, and there are plenty of them, with good coverage of club affairs. Excellent value at £1.50, and undoubtedly one of the best programmes in its Division.

TORQUAY UNITED FC

Founded: 1898 **Admitted to League**: 1927
Former Name(s): Torquay Town (1898-1910)
Ground Address: Plainmoor Ground, Torquay TQ1 3PS
Phone Number: (01803) 328666

TECHNICAL INFORMATION

Size: 239mm x 168mm
Nº of Pages: 32
Price: £1.50
% Full Colour: 50%
% Adverts: 28.12%
% Content: 71.88%
Total Price per Page: 4.69p
Price per Page of Content: 6.52p
Printer: Kingfisher Print & Design Limited, Totnes
Editor: A. Sandford
Club Shop Phone: (01803) 328666

PROGRAMME MONTHLY REVIEW COMMENTS:

A disappointingly light-weight programme from TORQUAY UNITED, with quite prominent commerical and advertising content. Design is bright and attractive, with the non-full colour pages once again cleverly composed. The main complaint is a shortage of reading material, although the features are varied, opinionated and very readable. There is the basis of an excellent programme, with room for improvement.

TOTTENHAM HOTSPUR FC

Founded: 1882 **Admitted to League**: 1908
Former Name(s): Hotspur FC (1882-1885)
Ground Address: White Hart Lane, 748 High Road, Tottenham, London N17 0AP
Phone Number: (0181) 365-5000

TECHNICAL INFORMATION

Size: 240mm x 165mm
Nº of Pages: 48
Price: £1.80
% Full Colour: 100%
% Adverts: 20.83%
% Content: 79.17%
Total Price per Page: 3.25p
Price per Page of Content: 4.74p
Printer: Total Graphics
Editor: John Fennelly
Club Shop Phone: (0181) 808-5959

PROGRAMME MONTHLY REVIEW COMMENTS:

It goes without saying that the TOTTENHAM HOTSPUR programme will be colourful, glossy, substantial and full of good reading; and this season's programme does not disappoint in any of these areas. Design is a lot less fussy than before, and will appeal more to some as a consequence. The programme is not over-burdened with reading matter – a trend which is becoming widespread as other club media expand.

TRANMERE ROVERS FC

Founded: 1881 **Admitted to League**: 1921
Former Name(s): Belmont FC
Ground Address: Prenton Park, Prenton Road West, Birkenhead L42 9PN
Phone Number: (0151) 608-0371

TECHNICAL INFORMATION

Size: 240mm x 170mm
Nº of Pages: 40
Price: £1.50
% Full Colour: 100%
% Adverts: 25%
% Content: 75%
Total Price per Page:
3.75p
Price per Page of Content:
5.00p
Printer: Tech Litho
Editor: None Credited
Club Shop Phone:
(0151) 608-0371

PROGRAMME MONTHLY REVIEW COMMENTS:

The TRANMERE ROVERS programme has been refined over the years into a polished, professional and highly attractive production. This season's style is very high on colour and bright design, preferring small chunks of features and information to more wordy features. There is a good level of reading matter, but not as much as before, and one is conscious of the predominance of design and pictorial coverage. "Rovers Review" remains an excellent programme, and while none of its predecessors looked as nice, they undoubtedly contained more features.

WALSALL FC

Founded: 1888 **Admitted to League**: 1892
Former Name(s): Walsall Town Swifts FC (1888-1895)
Ground Address: Bescot Stadium, Bescot Crescent, Walsall, W. Mids. WS1 4SA
Phone Number: (01922) 22791

TECHNICAL INFORMATION

Size: 228mm x 159mm
Nº of Pages: 32
Price: £1.50
% Full Colour: 25%
% Adverts: 21.87%
% Content: 78.13%
Total Price per Page: 4.68p
Price per Page of Content: 6.00p
Printer: Permandos A&M Lichfield
Editor: Don Stanton
Club Shop Phone: (01922) 31072

PROGRAMME MONTHLY REVIEW COMMENTS:

The WALSALL programme is as delightful as usual, and the club are to be highly commended for continuing with Don Stanton's long-standing format. There are 48 page, large-size Premiership programmes which contain a great deal less reading matter than this packed and compact issue. Never mind the width – feel the quality.

WATFORD FC

Founded: 1891 **Admitted to League**: 1920
Former Name(s): Formed by amalgamation of West Herts FC & St. Mary's FC
Ground Address: Vicarage Road Stadium, Watford WD1 8ER
Phone Number: (01923) 496000

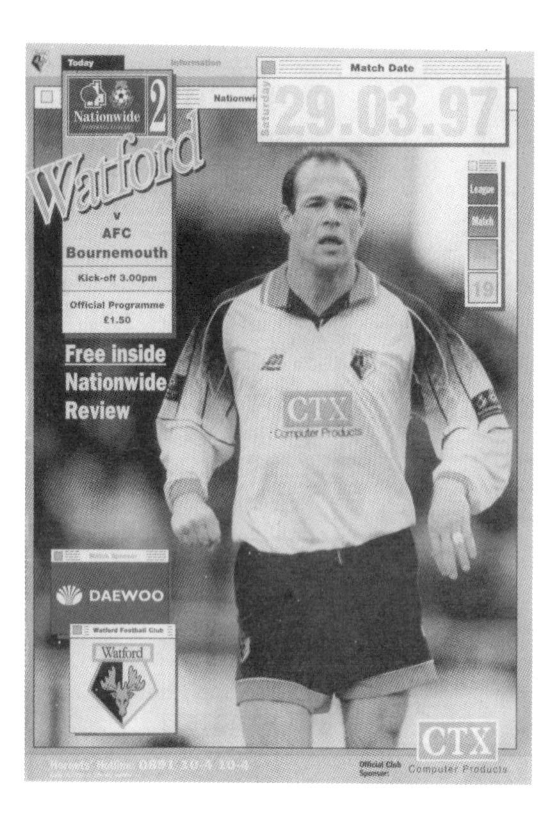

TECHNICAL INFORMATION

Size: 240mm x 170mm
Nº of Pages: 32
Price: £1.50
% Full Colour: 100%
% Adverts: 21.87%
% Content: 78.13%
Total Price per Page: 4.68p
Price per Page of Content: 6.00p
Printer: Alpine Press, Kings Langley
Editor: None credited
Club Shop Phone: (01923) 496005

PROGRAMME MONTHLY REVIEW COMMENTS:

WATFORD have retained their widely-admired and long-standing format, but have updated the design to emulate a computer-screen as standard page design. The result verges on the over-whelming, with an extremely packed production. This is undoubtedly value for money, despite there being "only" 32 pages, with plenty of features and club items keeping the fans fully informed.

WEST BROMWICH ALBION FC

Founded: 1879 **Admitted to League**: 1888
Former Name(s): West Bromwich Strollers (1879-1880)
Ground Address: The Hawthorns, Halfords Lane, West Bromwich, West Midlands, B71 4LF
Phone Number: (0121) 525-8888

TECHNICAL INFORMATION

Size: 244mm x 167mm
Nº of Pages: 40
Price: £1.50
%Full Colour: 100%
% Adverts: 17.5%
% Content: 82.5%
Total Price per Page: 3.75p
Price per Page of Content: 4.55p
Printer: Paper Plane Publishing Limited
Editor: None credited
Club Shop Phone: (0121) 525-2145

PROGRAMME MONTHLY REVIEW COMMENTS:

A bit of a curate's egg from WEST BROMWICH ALBION, with some substantial articles and features, and some disappointing-looking pages, usually where advertising/commercial items prevail. It is a good, solid, colourful programme, with plenty to read including some nice supporter-related features. If anything, the programme is possibly over-designed without a common identity across the pages. This does not portray the otherwise worthy content to best effect.

West Ham United FC

Founded: 1895 **Admitted to League**: 1919
Former Name(s): Thames Iron Works FC
Ground Address: Boleyn Ground, Green Street, Upton Park, London E13 9AZ
Phone Number: (0181) 548-2748

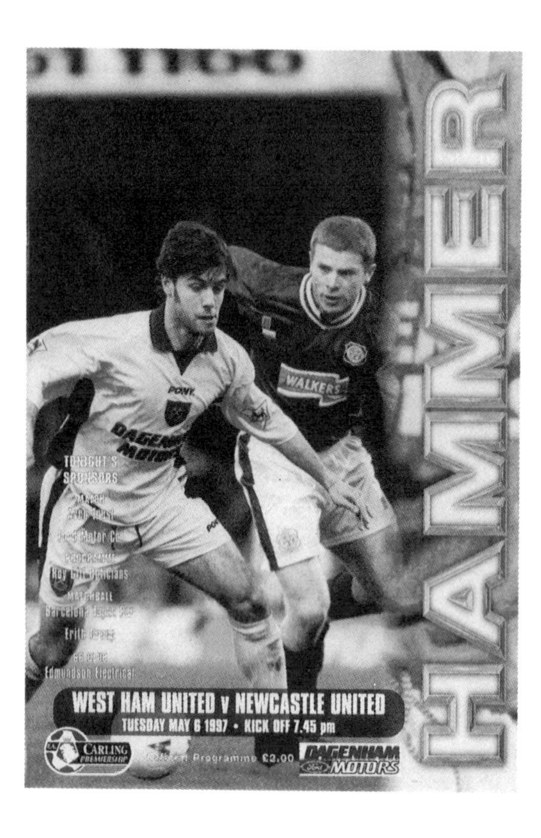

TECHNICAL INFORMATION

Size: 240mm x 165mm
Nº of Pages: 48
Price: £2.00
% Full Colour: 100%
% Adverts: 25%
% Content: 75%
Total Price per Page: 4.17p
Price per Page of Content: 5.56p
Printer: M Press (Sales) Limited
Editor: Peter Stewart
Club Shop Phone: (0181) 548-2748

PROGRAMME MONTHLY REVIEW COMMENTS:

Similar format to last year at WEST HAM UNITED and no harm in that. A thoroughly good programme packed with features and club news, and very attractively presented with predominant use of the famous claret and light blue colours. Plenty to read, albeit at a price. This is up with the best in the Premiership, and is once again a programme to delight Hammers fans.

WIGAN ATHLETIC AFC

Founded: 1932 **Admitted to League**: 1978
Former Name(s): None
Ground Address: Springfield Park, Wigan, Lancs. WN6 7BA
Phone Number: (01942) 244433

TECHNICAL INFORMATION

Size: 237mm x 159mm
Nº of Pages: 32
Price: £1.50
% Full Colour: 100%
% Adverts: 25%
% Content: 75%
Total Price per Page: 4.69p
Price per Page of Content: 6.25p
Printer: Mercer Print, Accrington
Editor: None credited
Club Shop Phone: (01942) 244433

PROGRAMME MONTHLY REVIEW COMMENTS:

Pleasant looking programme from WIGAN ATHLETIC nicely designed, colourful and well presented. Content, sadly, is a little on the brief side, although the use of available space cannot be faulted. The comparative lack of pages and hefty advertising/commercial coverage give little room for manoeuvre.

WIMBLEDON FC

Founded: 1889 **Admitted to League**: 1977
Former Name(s): Wimbledon Old Centrals FC (1889-1905)
Ground Address: Selhurst Park, London SE25 6PY
Phone Number: (0181) 771-2233

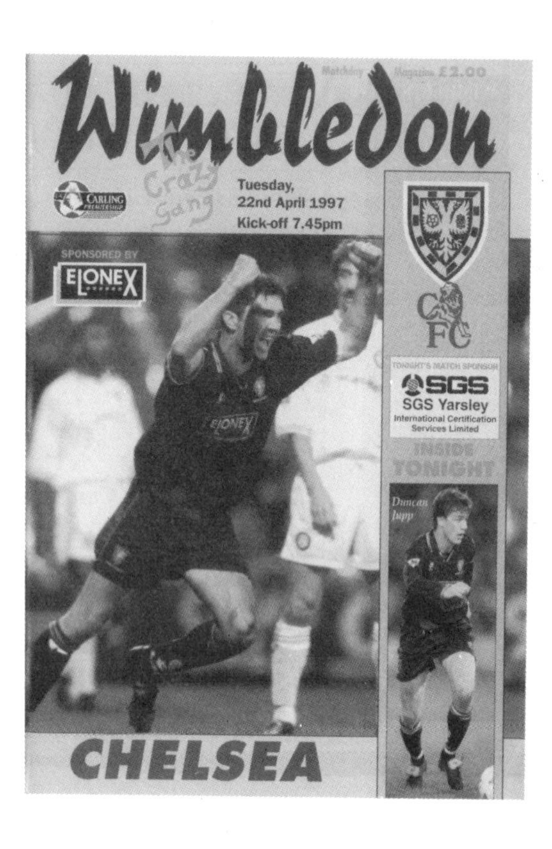

TECHNICAL INFORMATION

Size: 239mm x 167mm
Nº of Pages: 48
Price: £2.00
% Full Colour: 100%
% Adverts: 20.83%
% Content: 79.17%
Total Price per Page: 4.17p
Price per Page of Content: 5.26p
Printer: Sports & Leisure Print Limited
Editor: Reg Davies
Club Shop Phone: (0181) 653-5584

PROGRAMME MONTHLY REVIEW COMMENTS:

The "Crazy Gang" from WIMBLEDON have retained their primary colour-based programme style, with ample space for plenty of reading matter and substantial features on the club, which does well to compensate for its limited community involvement as they lodge at Selhurst Park. Well up to Premiership standards, without trying anything fancy.

WOLVERHAMPTON WANDERERS FC

Founded: 1877 **Admitted to League**: 1888
Former Name(s): St. Luke's FC & The Wanderers FC (amalgamated in 1880)
Ground Address: Molineux Ground, Waterloo Road, Wolverhampton WV1 4QR
Phone Number: (01902) 655000

TECHNICAL INFORMATION

Size: 244mm x 165mm
Nº of Pages: 48
Price: £1.50
% Full Colour: 100%
% Adverts: 25%
% Content: 75%
Total Price per Page: 3.12p
Price per Page of Content: 4.17p
Printer: Precision Colour Printing, Telford
Editor: None Credited
Club Shop Phone: (01902) 687032

PROGRAMME MONTHLY REVIEW COMMENTS:

WOLVERHAMPTON WANDERERS have produced a quite stunning looking programme this season with a distinctive and attractive design. If there has to be a quibble, it is that text gets a little bit lost amidst the sumptuous design and colour photography, particularly in the second half. That apart, this has the look and feel of a Premiership programme.

WREXHAM FC

Founded: 1873 **Admitted to League**: 1921
Former Name(s): None
Ground Address: Racecourse Ground, Mold Road, Wrexham, Clwyd LL11 2AH
Phone Number: (01978) 262129

TECHNICAL INFORMATION

Size: 229mm x 162mm
Nº of Pages: 40
Price: £1.50
% Full Colour: 100%
% Adverts: 22.5%
% Content: 77.5%
Total Price per Page: 3.75p
Price per Page of Content: 4.84p
Printer: Engraving Services Ltd., Manchester
Editor: D. Roberts, G. Parry, P. Jones
Club Shop Phone: (01978) 352536

PROGRAMME MONTHLY REVIEW COMMENTS:

How do they do it? Every year we praise WREXHAM for improving an already outstanding-programme; and each successive year they confound expectations by making their programme even better. This is truly an outstanding programme, which now compares in size, colour, design and price, with anything in the Premiership, yet keeps advertising at bay. It is no exaggeration to say that this is as good as anything in the country – if not better. The level of reading matter, and quality of presentation, makes this outstanding value for money.

WYCOMBE WANDERERS FC

Founded: 1884 **Admitted to League**: 1993
Former Name(s): None
Ground Address: Adams Park, Hillbottom Road, Sands, High Wycombe, Bucks.
Phone Number: (01494) 472100

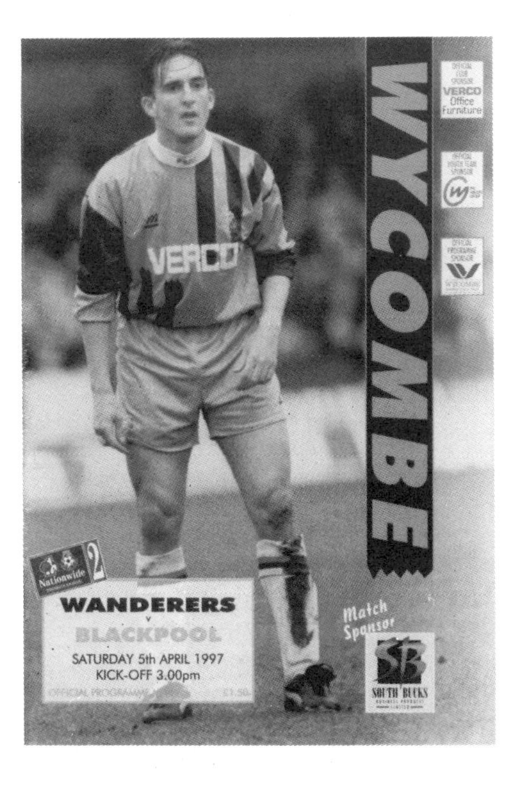

TECHNICAL INFORMATION

Size: 229mm x 158mm
Nº of Pages: 40
Price: £1.50
% Full Colour: 100%
% Adverts: 42.5%
% Content: 57.5%
Total Price per Page: 3.75p
Price per Page of Content: 6.52p
Printer: P.K. Graphics, High Wycombe
Editor: Adrian Wood
Club Shop Phone: (01494) 472100

PROGRAMME MONTHLY REVIEW COMMENTS:

WYCOMBE WANDERERS have finally shaken off the last vestiges of non-league-looking programmes with a more polished production this season. Design may still not be to the best of everyone's taste, but this is a colourful and bright production, with a very high level of reading, which is invariably informative and authoritative. The good news is that there is still room for improvement.

YORK CITY FC

Founded: 1922	**Admitted to League**: 1929
Former Name(s): None	
Ground Address: Bootham Crescent, York YO3 7AQ	
Phone Number: (01904) 624447	

TECHNICAL INFORMATION

Size: 245mm x 165mm
Nº of Pages: 32
Price: £1.50
% Full Colour: 100%
% Adverts: 40.62%
% Content: 59.38%
Total Price per Page: 4.69p
Price per Page of Content: 7.89p
Printer: Maxiprint, York
Editor: None credited
Club Shop Phone: (01904) 645941

PROGRAMME MONTHLY REVIEW COMMENTS:

A pleasant production from YORK CITY, with 12 black-and-white pages nicely disguised by over-printing on pre-printed colour. Plenty to read, with close printing making the most of an unpromising allocation of available non-advertising pages. Design suffers a little as a consequence, but this is a much improved programme that will surely find favour with the club's programme buying support.

SOCCER BOOKS LIMITED
72 ST. PETER'S AVENUE
CLEETHORPES
N.E. LINCOLNSHIRE
DN35 8HU

Phone (01472) 696226
Fax (01472) 698546

Web site: http://www.soccer-books.co.uk
e-mail: info@soccbook.demon.co.uk

BACK NUMBERS

We still have the undermentioned publications available post free at the prices shown. There are very few remaining copies of some of these titles so, please, order any that you require without delay to avoid disappointment.

Year	TITLE	Price	Qty	Order Value	
1992	The Supporters' Guide to Football League Clubs 1993	£4.99			
1992	The Supporters' Guide to Scottish Football 1993	£3.99			
1993	The Supporters' Gde. to Premier & Football League Clubs 1994	£4.99			
1993	The Supporters' Guide to Scottish Football 1994	£4.99			
1993	The Supporters' Guide to Non-League Football 1994	£4.99			
1993	The Supporters' Guide to Welsh Football 1994	£4.99			
1994	The Supporters' Gde. to Premier & Football League Clubs 1995	£4.99			
1994	The Supporters' Guide to Scottish Football 1995	£4.99			
1994	The Supporters' Guide to Non-League Football 1995	£4.99			
1994	The Supporters' Guide to Welsh Football 1995	£4.99			
1995	The Supporters' Gde. to Premier & Football League Clubs 1996	£4.99			
1995	The Supporters' Guide to Scottish Football 1996	£4.99			
1995	The Supporters' Guide to Non-League Football 1996	£4.99			
1995	The Supporters' Guide to Welsh Football 1996	£4.99			
1995	The Supporters' Guide to Football Programmes 1996	£4.99			
1996	The Supp. Guide to Premiership & Football League Clubs 1997	£4.99			
1996	The Supporters' Guide to Scottish Football 1997	£4.99			
1996	The Supporters' Guide to Non-League Football 1997	£4.99			
1996	The Supporters' Guide to Welsh Football 1997	£4.99			
1996	The Supporters' Guide to Irish Football 1997	£4.99			
1996	The Supporters' Guide to Football Programmes 1997	£4.99			